God's GRACE for Your Career

ENDORSEMENTS

Most of us don't stumble across burning bushes when we want to know our next career move. But that doesn't mean God hasn't given us all we need to align our daily work with his greater purposes. **God's GRACE For Your Career** is full of industry recognised tools, real-life stories and biblical reflection that will help you understand how your life, your faith and your work can better fit together.

Tim Yearsley, Head of Innovation, LICC

Katie Conley merges her many years of experience as a career counsellor with her Christian faith to bring a clear, relevant and accessible guide to enable people of all backgrounds to know and be pleased with their gifts, relationships, abilities, curiosity and experiences – that is G.R.A.C.E. Each chapter comes with case studies, parables, prayers and exercises to help the reader uncover these qualities. The book is likely to appeal to people who perhaps have lost their sense of purpose or "why". I love Katie's early story about a son who lost his way in life and returns home, expecting to be admonished by his father. Instead, he is given compassion which leads to self belief and a fresh start. As career counsellors, that is very much what we try to do for and with our clients. Katie has done a great job to communicate this through a particular lens, but one which has universal application.

Rob Nathan, Founder and CEO Career Counselling Services

This book is a little gem full of Katie's own heart and passion for each person to thrive. I love the way that she emphasises God's grace as she seeks to help us find career paths that reflect who He has made us to be. Full of stories and tools to help with career choices, I can see this being a helpful resource to many in a changing world. So glad to have been able to be part of this story in a small way.

Ruth Rice, Director, Renew Wellbeing

Katie's book combines her considerable personal experience and coaching models with interviews and biblical examples to provide an outstanding framework for anyone looking for more purpose in their career. Whether you are currently at a career crossroads, stuck in a rut or thriving, the thoughtful activities in each chapter help you to prayerfully consider what God's purpose for your career could be. Wherever you are currently working and whatever that involves, this book will help you to live the more purposeful life that we are all seeking.

Matt Parfitt, Founder & CEO, Grace Enterprises

I loved the focus on the Abilities section of the book and how these make you truly unique in the world. Katie helps you take a journey into your talents, skills and strengths to understand how you can make a difference and be happy. Each area has really easy and enjoyable exercises to help you discover your uniqueness, so be prepared to put in a bit of work around self-reflection – it will be worth it. She uses her strengths of Mission and Narrator to help you have a lightbulb moment in your own strengths and practically guides you towards purposeful action that's right for you.

Trudy Bateman, Director of Strengths Profile©

Katie has drawn many threads together in her wonderful "doing life before God Manual" as I am going to rename it. Specifically, what Katie does well is to synthesize wisdom from the Bible with wisdom from the world of career counselling and other fields related to better understanding our working lives, skills, dreams and aspirations. Packed full of practical tools and real-life examples of others who have drawn close to God and understood themselves more clearly as a result and the works He has prepared in advance for them to do. The book uses the word GRACE as both an acronym and an overarching theme that runs throughout the text. Our world and we as people need constant reminding of the grace of God and this book does this wonderfully well.

Stuart Palmer, Founder Director of BizMin

As a teenager, with no church background, I committed to following Jesus. Whatever He wanted me to do with my life I'd do it. But how would I know? I'm embarrassed to admit that after the absence of angels and trumpets, I'd flip open the Bible and read the first verse my eyes fell upon. Surely there'd be a career communicated directly from heaven? Well, if you want a more mature and grounded approach to discerning your next steps, Katie's book is excellent. Rooted in the wisdom of scripture, but also in lived human experience, it offers you many tools to help you follow God's lead. Katie helpfully breaks down the false dichotomy between "my ideas" and "God's ideas," and empowers you to fully embrace who you are made to be. There are personal stories, exercises, and encouragements to notice not just your own passions and gifts, but where the Spirit might be nudging you forward to use them. A book like this is long awaited in the Church, and much needed. You'll find it helpful whatever stage you are at, and I'm confident it will bring God's peace to your decision making.

Frances Finn, Priest and Broadcaster

What a joy it's been to read and use **God's GRACE for Your Career**. Reading Katie's own experience and wisdom along with the testimonies of others and the powerful sharing from the Bible has been highly insightful and inspirational. The skilful presentation of Katie's GRACE framework with opportunities for practical exercises and reflection has made it empowering and enjoyable. Whilst it has affirmed many parts of my own career journey as I've sought to meld my faith and every day work it has also challenged me to continue exploring what more and/or what else, with the comfort of knowing that God's grace is sufficient for me (2 Cor 12:9). I'd highly recommend it for anyone seeking God's purpose in their life or just needing a refresh on their working life.

Marjory Mair, Leadership and Team Coach at Marjory Mair Associates

God's GRACE for Your Career

Rediscover Your Purpose At Work

Katie Conley

Published: May 2023 Ladey Adey Publications, Ancaster, Lincolnshire UK.

ISBN: 978-1-913579-53-1(Paperback).
ISBN: 978-1-913579-54-8(E- Publication).

British Library Cataloguing-in-Publication Data.
A catalogue record for this book is available from
The British Library.

Cover Picture by Peter Gray, Big Appetite Illustration.

Illustrations by Mark Conley.

Photographs, including back cover by Gemma Wilks.

Please feel free to leave a review on Amazon for Katie.

DEDICATION

'Let us then approach God's
throne of grace with confidence,
so that we may receive mercy and find
grace to help us in our time of need'.

(Hebrews 4:16)

This book is dedicated to anyone who feels a bit lost at work, or who has a nagging feeling that there is more for their career but they're not sure what it is or where to find it.

May you know God's blessing and provision for your career and may you meet with Him as you explore the **GRACE** *He has given you for your career.*

Grace comes into the soul,
as the morning sun into the world;
first a dawning;
then a light;
and at last the sun
in his full and excellent brightness.

Thomas Adams

CONTENTS

AMAZING GRACE .... **xi**

INTRODUCTION .... **xiii**

Chapter One: GIFTS **3**

- Your Natural Gifts 5
- Your Personality 11
- Your Dreams 20
- Your Spiritual Gifts 26

Chapter Two: RELATIONSHIPS **37**

- Your Relationship With God 39
- Your Trusted Friends 53
- Your Wider Network 57
- Your Role Models 64

Chapter Three: ABILITIES **75**

- Your Talents 77
- Your Skills 83
- Your Strengths 93

Chapter Four: CURIOSITIES **109**

- Your Education 113
- Your Knowledge 117
- Your Interests 124
- Your Compassion 129
- Your Inner Wisdom 138
- Your Revelations From God 143

Chapter Five: EXPERIENCES **155**

- Your Career Journey 157
- Your Achievements 167
- Your Fruit 187
- Your Blessings 194
- Your Values 202

Chapter Six: GOD'S GRACE FOR YOU **213**

Kingdom Values.. 216
Your Grace Unwrapped.. 225
Your Career Blueprint.. 230
Your Career Purpose.. 238

EPILOGUE **243**

APPENDICES AND NOTES **245**

Appendix One: SPIRITUAL GIFTS:
SELF-ASSESSMENT CHECKLIST.......................... 247

Appendix Two: STRENGTH DEFINITIONS
FROM CAPPFINITY: STRENGTHS PROFILE©. 263

Appendix Three: BIBLE VERSES FOR KINGDOM
VALUES.. 265

Appendix Four: LIST OF ACTIVITIES.................... 275

ACKNOWLEDGEMENTS **277**

REFERENCES AND NOTES **281**

ABOUT THE AUTHOR.. **291**

INDEX.. **297**

YOUR NOTES.. **301**

A PRAYER FOR YOUR CAREER **306**

AMAZING GRACE

Amazing grace how sweet the sound
That saved a wretch like me
I once was lost, but now I'm found
Was blind but now I see

'Twas grace that taught my heart to fear
And grace my fears relieved
How precious did that grace appear
The hour I first believed

Through many dangers, toils, and snares
I have already come
'Tis grace has brought me safe thus far
And grace will lead me home

When we've been here ten thousand years
Bright, shining as the sun
We've no less days to sing God's praise
Than when we first begun

Amazing grace how sweet the sound
That saved a wretch like me
I once was lost, but now I'm found
Was blind but now I see

John Newton (1725–1807)

And then, what is grace? Grace is love.
But grace is not love simply, and purely, and alone.
Grace and love are, in their innermost essence,
one and the same thing.

Alexander Whyte

INTRODUCTION

'May the grace of the Lord Jesus
be with God's holy people.'
(Revelations 22:21 NLT)

God's **GRACE** is extraordinary. I hadn't realised quite how extraordinary until I felt inspired to write a book about careers for Christians. As a career coach, I realised my clients long to understand their career 'purpose' and to have meaning in their work. There are many resources to help people find purpose in their careers, but as I reviewed these resources, I felt there was a 'God-sized' hole in them. I wanted to develop some ideas which helped people explore their careers from God's perspective, to help them pray about their careers and consider career ideas within a Christian framework.

This realisation set me on a journey to write this book, and here it is fully inspired by God! He gave me the **GRACE** acronym during a prayer session when I developed the book outline as a mind map.

G for the **Gifts** God has given you, both natural and spiritual.

R for the **Relationships** you have with God and other people.

A for your **Abilities**; comprising your talents, skills and strengths.

C for your **Curiosities** about the world, which provide clues for your career choices.

E for your **Experiences**, understanding God uses everything, both good and bad.

My inspiration comes from the story of the Prodigal Son (Luke 15:11-32) which has much to teach us about God's grace. The younger son has strayed from his father and gone his own way, and his father lets him go. He gives the younger son his inheritance, the gifts, abilities, curiosities and lets him experience life without a relationship with his father.

Read the story and you'll know what happens; the younger son squanders his inheritance, he wastes it and uses it up until he is destitute, the lowest of the low, only able to eke out a meagre living feeding pigs and cleaning styes. He knows he is missing out on the life he should have had. He knows there is a better way to live. When he has reached rock bottom he decides to go home, to return to his father.

Then an amazing thing happens. His father is waiting and watching for his younger son. When he sees him, he is filled with compassion and picks up the corners of his outer garment and runs to meet his long-lost son and embraces him. The father reinstates his son, gives him clothes to wear, a ring for his finger, and sandals for his feet, followed by a sumptuous feast.

This is a wonderful story demonstrating God's grace. The son has lost his way in life and is returning home, expecting a lukewarm greeting, and hoping to work as a servant. He is bowled over by the unconditional and wholehearted greeting he is offered. His father longs to restore everything his son has lost and immediately reinstates him in the family.

Do you feel you have gone your own way and you are a bit lost in your career? Do you wonder what you are doing or where you are going? Do you sense God has something better for your career?

Then, return to God. Seek Him out and you will find He is ready and waiting with His unique package of **GRACE** for your career, ready to fill you with a sense of purpose for the work He has planned for you.

As you read the end of the story of the Prodigal Son, you'll notice there is another brother, an older brother who has stayed at home working in the family business. Although he is not happy about the merciful treatment his younger brother receives, his father's compassion extends to him as well, "My son", the father said, "You are always with me, and everything I have is yours" (Luke 15:31). He too has access to everything his father has.

Do you feel you have been on the career treadmill for a while? Do you feel stressed or burnt out despite doing what God wants in your career? Take some time to be refreshed by understanding the unique package of **GRACE** God has for your career.

Here is a place to explore the gifts He has given you, review your career experiences, understand your values and consider what God might have planned for your future.

God's GRACE for My Career

I became a believing Christian at a time of career transition in my life. I was 32 years old with two small children, having left my career job to set up my own business working from home. In a quiet moment, I picked up a copy of *Time Magazine* and read an article about Abraham which explained he was the forefather, or the Patriarch, of the three main religions, Judaism, Christianity and Islam. I was both intrigued and confused. It wasn't long after the Twin Towers had been attacked in New York[1], which I remember watching with shock and horror in my office whilst still at work. I couldn't understand why people whose religion had the same root, and seemed to worship the same God, could attack each other. Why was there so much strife between them? It puzzled me deeply and I wanted to find out more. Despite going to Church as a child and throughout my school days, I didn't really have a fully formed concept of God, so I decided to investigate the source documents and find out for myself.

Many years ago, my best friend from university had given me a Bible for a birthday present. I found it on my bookshelf, blew the cobwebs off and started at the beginning; Genesis Chapter 1 Verse 1. I have to say, I enjoyed the creation stories, but I didn't understand them at all. I thought, *"These stories are great, but I'm not sure what they mean?"* Being impatient, I decided to jump to the Gospels and as I read the stories of Jesus and the words He spoke I became amazed. I remember feeling astonished by who He said He was, the miracles He performed and the love He demonstrated.

"Wouldn't it have been incredible to have been alive when Jesus walked the earth? Wouldn't it have been amazing to have known Him?", I questioned in awe. Then I realised; the whole point of Jesus' death on the cross and His resurrection was so I could know Him today because He is alive. It was as if a light bulb was turned on for me. Then as I was thinking about this, I read Matthew 5:15 which says, people don't light a lamp and then hide it away, they put it where other people can see the light. It was as if God was saying, *"If you believe this, if you believe in me, stand up and be counted."* This might seem a bit weird, but I heard a voice in my heart, saying the words, *"Go to Church!"* The voice wasn't inside me and it wasn't audible. It was like a consciousness which I heard in my soul. I knew it wasn't me, it was God. There's no other

way for me to describe or account for it.

"Go to Church!" Well, I didn't want to go to Church at all. I thought it would be boring, tedious and really uncool. Then it occurred to me, Jesus was obedient to God and despite His pleading in the Garden of Gethsemane, He went willingly to his death on the cross (Matthew 26:36-46). If Jesus was obedient in His time of deep crisis then I could be obedient in this one small thing I didn't want to do - I would go to Church.

The following Sunday, I crept into the back of my local Anglican Church two minutes before the service started and I can honestly say I haven't looked back since. I found a place where I was warmly welcomed, where I was allowed to be myself, where I was allowed to ask questions and to explore my blossoming faith. A place where I felt as if God was speaking directly to me through the songs we sang, the words of the sermon (yes, really) and through the prayers we prayed. A faith family I could really belong to.

Becoming a Christian in my 30s, already immersed in a career as an independent learning and development consultant to the Film and TV industry, was a bit of a shock! Up to this point I had a vague belief in God, as a 'Being', way off and remote and of not much relevance to my daily life. I had no understanding or knowledge of a God who knew me profoundly in a very personal way. I was deeply moved when I realized just how much He cared for me, how much He loved me, He had a plan for me, and I began to experience His grace for me.

Life was very busy with young children and a business to run but when I became a Christian my whole perspective shifted. It felt as though I was walking on air whilst at the same time having an acute awareness I was not perfect, in any way, shape or form. I longed to tell people about my faith but didn't know how to explain it or if people would believe me. I delved enthusiastically into an Alpha course (Introduction to Christianity course[2]) my church was running and was back as a 'Helper' the following year. I had a deep desire to learn more and more about Jesus.

Becoming a regular worshipper at my local church I met a wonderful businessman who explained he had made Jesus the Senior Partner in his business. This seemed like an amazing idea and so I too made Jesus a Senior Partner. He has proved to be very gentle, very wise, and very patient with me. As I walked the tightrope of feast and famine as a self-employed consultant, I discovered time and time again Jesus wanted me to trust Him for work and in fact, His plans are so much better than mine!

In 2008, during the recession, most of my work dried up. I had a third child now. I was content being a stay-at-home Mum, whilst at the same time completing a Certificate in Discipleship (Certificate in Theology), running a home group[3] for Mums and Toddlers and overseeing the other home groups. God then led me to do some preaching in church. Later on, I became involved in running Alpha courses and leading two more home groups, having encouraged someone else to take on the Mums and Toddlers home group.

Walking alongside other Christians, discipling them had become a main focus in my life. Then God opened the door for me to work one day a week with a small company recommended by a friend. I longed to tell my colleagues about Jesus but felt inhibited by the workplace culture and constrained by the employment contract. I began to pray,

"Father God, should I start up my own business again?" His answer came through an ex-colleague who wanted to work with me on a consultancy contract. We bid for the work, were successful and I was back working for myself and thriving again.

I firmly believe this was all part of God's plan. Despite being unable to share my faith when I was employed, I gained experience of working with a variety of different businesses which really helped when I worked for myself again. It had given me the confidence to go back to work having had some time out as a full-time Mum.

The gifts and talents God has given me for my career mean I am really suited to working for myself, using my entrepreneurial traits combined with my desire for autonomy alongside my skills and strengths whilst allowing for time to continue volunteering with my Church.

In 2016, I bid for work on a Leadership Programme and was awarded a contract to run one-to-one career development coaching sessions. I loved working individually with each person on a bespoke career plan, designed specifically around their development needs. People started to introduce me as career coach. Once again, I had been praying to God about the next stage of my career and I definitely felt a sense of His peace as I decided to focus on career coaching and searched for an accreditation programme. I also sensed His affirmation that my work as a career coach should have a Christian focus, be built on Kingdom of God values and offer a space for Christians to explore their career options.

I have been amazed, since then, at how God has opened doors for me to meet and work with other Christians. When I focus on Him, I have a sense of peace. I love the connections He makes. I feel a sense of deep satisfaction when I help people with their careers and see God's plan at work in their lives.

I am delighted to have written this book and have been blessed by the way God has inspired it. My prayer is for God to bless you and your careers through it too.

God's GRACE for Your Career

Psalm 139 was written by King David and describes how God watched over David when he was in his mother's womb. 'For you created my inmost being; you knit me together in my mother's womb. I praise you because I am fearfully and wonderfully made' (Psalm 139:13). Before he was even born, God 'knit him together'. This knitting is like beautiful delicate embroidery, carefully and skilfully woven, so all the intricacies of the body work together. God created you just as He planned with a unique package of gifts, talents skills and aptitudes which make up 'you'.

The uniqueness God has given you is packaged with **GRACE** and I have used this acronym to help you unpack what He has given you. This is not always a neat package of uniqueness. There are overlaps and gaps and sometimes it looks a bit messy. However, it is being skilfully woven by God, who sees the end result long before you do.

Yes! It's messy and different for everyone. It takes time to make sense of your individual knitting so you might find you spend more time in some chapters than others. You might spend considerable time pondering your natural gifts, or considering your dreams, or you might jump straight ahead to explore your values or see what's in your Vine of Curiosity.

Your career is individual to you. I share the view of Julia Yates, in her book *The Career Coaching Handbook,* 'If you think it is a career, then it is a career'.[4] Your career could be full time, part time, professional, vocational, paid, voluntary, progressive, or maybe even retired. The way you do your work is also individual to you, whether you are stacking shelves, feeding cattle or running a corporation, God has filled you with **GRACE** for your career. He can provide meaning to what you do when you understand the **GRACE** he has given you.

As you read through or dip in and out of this book, you will find prayers, Bible stories and verses, and interviews. I'll introduce you to David, a landscape garden designer; Maria, a secondary school teacher; Michelle, an actor; Sue, a doctor and Sheralyn, a lawyer and entrepreneur as they share details about their careers. They will pop up throughout the book along with Matt, a self-employed painter and decorator; Jane, an emotional and wellbeing consultant; Dewi, a managing director and Hanna, a cancer nurse specialist.

You'll also read interviews from Bruce, an author and e-learning expert; Mark, a company director; Ladey, author, speaker and publisher, Lisa, head of operations, and Natasha, a consultant, alongside other contributors including some of my career coaching clients. Their stories illustrate many of the **GRACE** elements detailed in this book.

Alongside this are activities to help you see your career from God's perspective. Ken Costa writes, 'The better we know ourselves, the more we can imagine what kind of work God might be calling us to.'[5] So, I invite you to get to know yourself better, to explore the **GRACE** God has given you for your career. I hope you will realise, as I have, God has been at work in your career effecting His plan through all the highs and lows, and His grace is more than enough.

Grace is God's undeserved love for us. It's His unconditional love. We cannot earn God's grace. It is His free gift, given to us through the death and resurrection of Jesus on the cross. We receive it when we return to God, when we repent, turn away from our sin, and put our faith in Jesus. Paul writes in Romans 10:9, 'If you declare with your mouth, "Jesus is Lord," and believe in your heart that God raised him from the dead, you will be saved'.

My prayer is you would be blessed as God reveals your own package of **GRACE**, for you to gather strands of gold in the knitting which makes up your personal embroidery and along the way you would discover God's blueprint and purpose for your current and future career.

Katie Conley

Prayer

Father God, thank You for the **GRACE** You have given me for my career. Guide me through Your Holy Spirit as I explore the Gifts, Relationships, Abilities, Curiosities and Experiences which make up the unique package of **GRACE** for my career.

In Jesus name, Amen.

GRACE

Gifts

Relationships

Abilities

Curiosities

Experiences

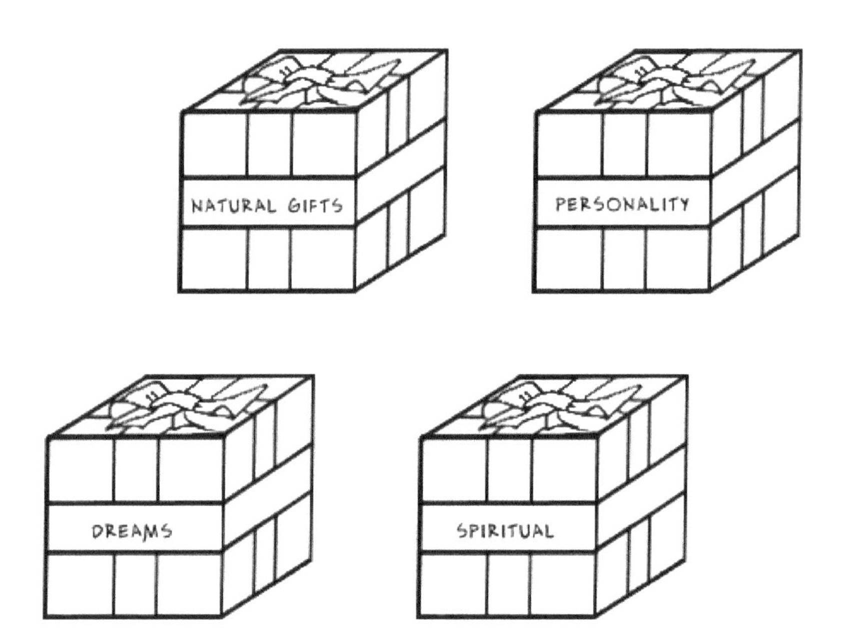
NATURAL GIFTS
PERSONALITY
DREAMS
SPIRITUAL

Chapter One: GIFTS

'Every good and perfect gift is from above,
coming down from the Father of the heavenly lights, who does not change like shifting shadows'.

(James 1:17)

Do you remember your excitement as a child in anticipation of presents under the Christmas tree, seeing one with your name on, and then unwrapping it to see what you've been given? This is the gift someone has chosen just for you. As a parent I love watching my children open the gifts I have chosen for them, gifts they wanted, gifts they weren't expecting and gifts which make them shout for joy. I bought my four-year-old son a Buzz Lightyear[1] costume and he literally wore it every day for the next six months! Remembering this still makes me smile.

This is how God feels about the gifts He has given you for your career. They are carefully selected to fit your character, personality and your inner self; and bring joy to your heart. Father God has wrapped these gifts up for you and longs to watch you unwrap them.

Of course, Christmas is in celebration of the birth of Jesus, and His birth was marked by the giving of gifts from the wise men. 'On coming to the house, they saw the child with His mother Mary, and they bowed down and worshipped Him. Then they opened their treasures and presented Him with gifts of gold, frankincense and myrrh' (Matthew 2:11).

These gifts were not an accident or given by mistake. They were gifts fit for a King. Gifts from exotic lands, not readily available in Bethlehem. They were chosen specifically for Jesus, by learned wise men who followed a star to find Him.

They understood He was born King of the Jews (Matthew 2:2) and chose gifts befitting this role; *'gold was a gift for royalty; frankincense a gift for deity; and myrrh was a spice used to anoint a body for burial,'*[2] indicating Jesus' humanity. They were carefully chosen just for Jesus.

In the same way, God has chosen gifts specifically for you, befitting the role He has in mind for you. Sometimes we find it hard to identify these gifts, let alone accept them, but I encourage you to take time to discover what they are.

In this chapter you'll start by exploring the gifts God gave you as a child, your **Natural Gifts.** These are the activities you find easy and come naturally to you. They are the building blocks of your abilities which you will explore more in Chapter Three: ABILITIES. You will consider your **Personality**, and the components God has used in making you who you are. Then you will dream **Dreams**! What dreams do you have for your career? Finally, you'll review your **Spiritual Gifts** and consider how God might want you to use them in your career.

Let's go on a journey together to unwrap the gifts God has given you. Gifts come in many shapes and sizes, and not just at Christmas! God will keep giving you gifts throughout your career.

Prayer

Father God thank You for all the gifts You have
given me – help me to find them and unwrap
them so I can use them for Your glory.
In Jesus name, Amen.

YOUR NATURAL GIFTS

'Each of you should use whatever gift you have received to serve others, as faithful stewards of God's grace in its various forms'.

(1 Peter 4:10)

David was out tending sheep in the pasture when God sent Samuel to anoint him as King (1 Samuel 16:11). I imagine David sitting on a little hillock, strumming his harp singing praises to God as the sheep grazed on the lush grass around him. I know this is probably an idealised view, the ground may well have been arid, and David may well have been trekking for miles to find water for the sheep, or tending to a lame sheep, or protecting them from wild animals, but the point is God had gifted David with some natural gifts. He was the youngest son, so he probably knew how to fend for himself, he loved singing and was good at playing the harp. Many of the Psalms in the Bible are credited to him. We read of his harp playing to soothe King Saul's temperament (1 Samuel 16:23). We know he wrote several of the Psalms, including the famous Psalm 23, The Lord is My Shepherd.

God looks at his heart (1 Samuel 16:7) and knows David's love for God, his love for the sheep, his courage in killing lions and bears who try to steal and kill the sheep (1 Samuel 17:34-36), and no doubt he is used to managing an unruly herd as they wander through the mountains and plains. This stands him in good stead for when he faces Goliath and later still for when he becomes King, dealing with matters of state, making decisions and protecting the people. The clues for his future skills and strengths were evident in his natural gifts as he tended to sheep as a shepherd. We will explore this in Chapter Three: ABILITIES.

David understood God had given him natural gifts when he was created in his mother's womb (Psalm 139:13). These gifts become evident in his childhood, as he played as a child, grew as a teenager looking after the sheep and then as he matured as an adult. It's the same with you and me.

Loving animals was something which came easily to me. When I was a toddler, my parents had a dog and I followed him around everywhere and learned to love him. I was the one who rushed to feed our guinea pigs each morning. When I was eight years old my family looked after a pony who was used for *Riding for the Disabled Association.*[3] He was a bad-tempered welsh mountain pony called *Winkey*, who was gentle as a dove with the disabled children but didn't want to be disturbed by me when he was eating fresh grass in the paddock. I remember my tears in the car on the first day I met him because he was so bad tempered, but by the end of the year we looked after him, I adored him.

When I was a teenager, we got a puppy, I was the one who got up in the middle of the night to comfort her as she settled into her new home. I was the one who would go horse riding come rain or shine, who won a prize for, *'loving her pony the most!'*

I still love animals, but what stands out for me looking back, is how good I was at building relationships. As a child, I found it easier to build relationships with animals, but as an adult, and with God's guidance I am happy to spend time building relationships with people. It feels effortless when I take the time to do this because I'm using the natural gift God has given me.

I used to love running everywhere as a child. I would always be running, just so I could get wherever I wanted to go more quickly. Today, I really don't enjoy running. In fact, I'll avoid running if I possibly can, but it's interesting looking back to understand why I ran so much.

It was the desire for results (to get where I was going!) which motivated me ... not a love of running. Even today, I chase after results in the way I work and manage my time, I'm not running from A to B, but I'm definitely motivated to work towards a goal. The clue was there when I was a child, even though it took looking back at all my childhood running as an adult, to identify what was going on.

David's Natural Gifts

I interviewed David, a landscape garden designer, and asked him what he loved to do when he was a child. This is what he said,

> *"We were always out playing a lot, playing football on the fields or just out all day enjoying nature really, being outdoors and being active. Nature was a big part of the primary school I went to. It had a farm, and we could look after the animals. There was a wood and I remember the whole of our class planting trees, in a group of three I planted a beech tree, and it's still there today. My teacher used to draw pictures on the board for us to copy, like a spider. She would draw it very carefully, including the detail of the legs and the body and the eyes. I used to love copying it and I realised I could draw, and a lot of the drawings I did were of nature and animals. I remember there was a display in the hall of about 10 pictures and eight of them were mine although nobody knew, which was quite funny really because I had just drawn them easily, it came naturally to me. Looking back now I feel like I would say*

God was in my drawing because he knew the natural gift in me. So that's quite humbling."

Maria's Natural Gifts

Maria, head of secondary school and modern languages co-ordinator, spoke of her love of reading as a child, and going to the local Library with her father,

> *"Dad used to take us to the Library and it was exciting; being able to choose five books to take home to read, and you couldn't make a wrong choice. I loved reading."*

Maria also went to ballet lessons, which she really enjoyed.

> *"I liked the classical music, the systematic and structured approach to dance, and later discovered all the terms were in French. Doing ballet was the first time I heard French words spoken, and as I prepared for ballet exams, I saw the French words written beside the ballet steps. I began to learn French at school and started to make the connections. So for me, it wasn't about visiting France, but encountering the language through an activity I loved, and this sowed the seeds for my future. I still love watching a ballet; the music really moves me and the dancer's skill and grace, and I still love words and different languages.*
>
> *As a teenager, I continued to learn French at school, along with German. At home, Mum used to dictate Spanish words for me to write letters to her sister in Spain. I didn't know Spanish then but it's quite phonetic. So, once I'd learnt certain sounds, I could write out the word she was sounding, even though I didn't understand their meanings."*

Maria went on to complete a BA Joint Honours in European Studies, with French and German at university. It's fascinating to see how her early love of the French language combined with her love of reading and words, her introduction to German at school and Spanish at home led to study choices which were a complete fit with her natural gifts. You can read more of her story in Chapter Five: EXPERIENCES.

Exploring the natural gifts God has given you starts by reviewing the patterns of things you used to do easily as a child. Then as you mature these natural gifts grow into abilities such as talents, skills and strengths, which we will explore further in Chapter Three: ABILITIES.

So I ask, "Tell me about your childhood?"

Activity 1:
What are Your Natural Gifts?

To help you find your natural gifts note down the things you used to enjoy doing. Use the questions below to prompt your memory.

- What did you really enjoy doing as a child? Did you like playing with friends, toys or on your own?
- What things were you naturally drawn to? This could be things like people, pets, the outdoors, music.
- Did you like music, sport, art, design, sewing, gardening, reading, writing, shopping, talking, watching, listening, building things, exploring technology? What other things did you like?

- What games did you play as a child? Hide and seek, tag, make believe, dressing up, on your own or with other people?
- What were your favourite toys? If you played with Lego®, did you prefer to make people or buildings? If you played with dolls or stuffed toys what did you do with them? Did you care for them or organise them?
- How did you spend your free time? Did you play outside or did you sit indoors colouring, reading and daydreaming?
- What would you be doing when you lost track of time? What were you good at? Try to remember specific times when this happened.

Ask God to remind you of anything you may have forgotten, and when you've exhausted list making, take a pause!

Then review your list and highlight any patterns, or anything which particularly resonates with you, and make a note of any key points.

You might not be doing these things anymore, but your natural gifts will give you clues about how God has gifted you naturally.

Prayer

Father God thank you for the natural gifts I was
born with, the things You gave me at birth,
the things I naturally find easy to do.
As I make a note of them now remind
me of anything I may have forgotten.

In Jesus name, Amen

YOUR PERSONALITY

'I praise You because I am fearfully and wonderfully made;
Your works are wonderful,
I know that full well'.

(Psalms 139:14)

God designed you to His own pattern, not anyone else's. He crafted your personality as an intrinsic part of who you are and how you respond to the world. Personality is 'the various aspects of a person's character which combine to make them different from other people'.[4] Your personality is unique to you and is made up of a myriad of qualities and characteristics which make you distinctively you.

When you understand your own personality this gives you clues about the type of work you are suited to. This is only a part of the unique package of **GRACE** God has for you. He is not limited in how He might use you, regardless of the personality He has gifted you with.

There are lots of different characters in the Bible. They all have different personalities which impact how they do the work God has called them to. Consider the twelve disciples, all charged with following Jesus, learning from Him and making His Name known. Each disciple approached this role in a different way depending on their personality.

Peter is a great example – he is forthright, daring, vocal and impetuous. When Jesus walks on water, it's Peter who steps out of the boat to meet Him (Matthew 14:28-29). It's Peter who passionately declares he will stand by Jesus when He's on trial and then denies Jesus (Matthew 26:69-75). It's Peter who is first out of the boat to see Jesus after the resurrection (John 21:7). His personality is the driving force in how he reacts to situations and later when he's called to be the leader of the emerging church (Matthew 16:18).

Next consider John. We learn about him from the letters he wrote and from his Gospel,[5] markedly different from the other three Gospels. In his Gospel, he focusses on the divinity of Jesus, the perspective of eternity, the miracles, the signs and wonders Jesus performed. John is a family man, son of Zebedee, brother of James, (Mark 1:19-20) and was entrusted with Jesus' mother Mary after His crucifixion (John 19:26-27). John focuses on relationship building, writing to *"my dear children"*, and *"dear friends"* (1 John 2:1, 2:7) exhorting us above all to love God and to love one another in obedience to Christ (John 15:12). The impression is of someone passionate about declaring the truth of who Jesus is.

Both these men were disciples of God used by God in similar roles, but with very different emphasis according to their personalities. So, you can see from this how God can use different personalities in similar roles. We all have a combination of different personality traits which may suit us for different careers. When you believe God has a specific plan for your career, He can make use of any personality in any situation He chooses!

For example, if you want to be a chef, you could be extravert or introvert, you could be bursting with creative ideas or enjoy the detail of using specific ingredients. However, if you are a researcher, it's likely your personality traits will be conducive to this type of work, such as being focused, detail driven, happy in your own company or maybe you love the thrill of a discovery. We are all uniquely made, and the aspects of one person's personality suited to being a researcher will not be equally the same as another researcher. Your personality is just one part of who God designed you to be.

Although the career choices you make are not just about your type of personality, it does help in your career search to understand your own personality since this often provides a good starting point. Psychologists over many years have developed personality questionnaires to help people understand their personality preferences, and often these personality profiling tools are used in recruitment and career development situations.

Bruce's Expert Thoughts on Your Personality

I spoke with Bruce, an e-learning expert and author, to find out more about personality profiling.

Bruce used to work for BT in a team of managers who used personality profiling to help people understand their preferred working styles. His work included assessment centres for graduates, management insight courses and situational leadership training. His favourite tool is the Myers Briggs Type Indicator, developed by Katherine Briggs and her daughter Isabel Myers which is based on initial theories developed by German psychologist, Carl Jung. There are 16 main profiles based on a combination of four scales of personality. These are assessed by completing a questionnaire designed to elicit focused results, with an infinitely variable scale for each profile.

The first scale assesses extraversion and introversion (E & I). This scale is about where you get your energy from and where you focus your attention. Bruce comments,

> *"If you found yourself in a beautiful woodland, surrounded by God's creatures, God's creation, and beautiful flowers, would you stand there and say,*

"This is brilliant, here I am on my own. No one's around. I'm loving this" or are you the sort of person who would say, "Well, this is great. But actually, I'd really like people to experience this with me to appreciate the joy it's bringing me. So I can share my joy with others"? If you're a person who would want to experience something with other people, and you tend to recharge with other people then you have a preference for extraversion, and you are likely to gain your energy from outward experiences with others. If you're someone with a preference for introversion, you're more likely to love spending your moment in creation on your own."

This is about your personal preferences. Maybe you like to spend time on your own as well as being with other people. You are probably somewhere along the variable scale between the extremes of extraversion and introversion, rather than being one or the other. This profile is about where you get your energy from. Some people thrive with other people, whereas others find their energy is restored when they are on their own.

The second scale is called sensing and intuition (S & N). This relates to how you find information and data, how you process it and whether you trust it or not. Bruce says,

"Imagine you get a new toy or gadget for Christmas, and it comes with an instruction book. Someone who's got a preference for sensing would probably read through the instruction book to find out what the gadget can do, whereas someone with a preference for intuition would want to get it out to play on it, get the buttons going and discover how it works. People with a sensing preference tend to focus on the presented facts, they like clarity of objectives. People with intuitive preference use their

imagination and hunches to envision the future.

Again, this is a sliding scale, but if you did imagine yourself on Christmas morning with a new gadget, I'm pretty sure you'll know if you have a sensing preference if you find yourself reading through the instructions or watching the informational video. If your first action is to switch the gadget on and just start figuring it out, it's likely your preference is for intuition."

The third scale is about thinking and feeling (T & F), which is about how you make decisions and judgements. Bruce uses the following example.

"Imagine you are in charge of an HR department, and you have to make a bunch of people redundant. If you are on the thinking end of the scale, you're likely to consider everything from the business impact, such as how losses will affect the work rosters. Are you going to have sufficient resources to fit into the departments, based on the number of people you had, and how many you're going to be left with? Or if you're on the feeling end of the scale you are more likely to make decisions about the impact of redundancies on what you know about the people involved such as 'this person's got family and this person is young and has got lots of capabilities so could easily find another job, another person could struggle to find a job.' So you would base decisions on your feelings about the people".

Obviously, there are laws and regulations governing redundancies and how people are selected, but the point Bruce is making is that the preference people have for making these decisions varies between their heart (the feelers) and their head (the thinkers), and of course the sliding scale between the two.

The fourth scale is judging and perceiving (J & P), how you deal with the environment around you and how you actually lead your life. For this scale, Bruce uses the idea of someone needing *"a really complicated report from you by five o'clock on Friday."* He says,

> *"People who have a preference for judgement, like closure and completion. They like to plan ahead and don't want surprises. So, what they tend to do is have their life structured in a way where they would make sure the report was delivered by five o'clock on Friday, or possibly earlier. They're organised and structured, and they've got other things they know they need to do as well. However, people with a preference for perception will view five o'clock Friday as actually meaning nine o'clock Monday morning, because we all know that none of the reports are going to get read over the weekend. So this means they don't actually need it done by five o'clock on Friday, they need it done by 9 o'clock Monday morning when work starts. This gives them the chance just to have another read through or another bit of a tweak because there may be some other results they find after Friday which they might want to drop into the report."*

People with a preference for judgement are likely to be focused on the deadline and what they need to do to meet it in time, whereas people with a preference for perception are likely to stay open minded about what might happen at the last minute. Bruce comments,

> *"People are influenced by being in a work setting and it's possible they are basing their choices on preferences influenced by their working environment rather than natural preferences, because of the way they are expected*

to behave or operate at work in their particular job role. This is important because it suggests there is an element of contextualisation on the results of your profile in how you respond to situations depending on your natural preference rather than any influenced preferences."

For the purposes of understanding your own personality profile, it's helpful to go back to being in the beautiful garden, listening to the birds singing, Bruce described, stripping away everyday distractions to consider how you would respond. He says,

"Do you want to share the experience, or do you want to keep enjoying it on your own? Is that your natural preference? In the mythical garden there's no risk, because you're on your own at the moment. What would you choose to do? Do you want to stay on your own? Okay, well, that was easy! That's your natural preference because it's not influenced by anything, you're not at work, you're not home. There's nobody around you. It's just you. And the decision is based on 'who am I really, when nobody's looking'?"

To find out about your own personality preferences you can use the free online questionnaire www.16personalities.com[6] based on the Myers Briggs Type Indicator.

When you download your report consider the things which really resonate with you and also make sense of what you know about yourself. Talk about what you find out with someone who knows you well. What do they think about your profile? How true to you is it?

Things to look for include how you gain energy, either from interacting with other people (extravert) or from introspectively reflecting on your own (introvert). If you love to be the life and soul of the party, then you're likely to be an extravert. Maybe you are refreshed and renewed by reading books, then you could be considered to be an introvert. This is not to say you can't be an extravert and love books too!

You will also discover how you like to process data or make sense of information. Some people like to deal with concrete concepts whereas others prefer to think in more abstract or conceptual terms. People make decisions in different ways, some basing decisions on how they feel and whether the decision is in line with their values. Others tend to rely on logical objective analysis to guide their decision making. When we come to taking action some of us like to plan and stick to a schedule whereas others prefer to be flexible relying on spontaneity. There are no hard and fast rules, it's all about uncovering who God made you to be.

The report on your personality profile generates a lot of information, so I suggest you make a note of anything which particularly resonates with you, which makes you say 'Yes', or which quickens in your spirit or heart. There shouldn't really be any surprises in the results from this questionnaire, but it is helpful to identify the personality traits you have which make you uniquely you!

The questionnaire also offers ideas about the types of careers which you might be suited for. I recommend you use these as initial sounding blocks rather than concrete options. As you read through this book, you will uncover a lot more information about your skills, interests, values and motivations which all play a part in your career choices.

My profile suggests I am an 'Assertive Defender'. As I read the report there were many things which connected with what I know about myself; although I am an introvert, I am naturally sociable. Some people might see this as an oxymoron, but the point I'm trying to make is God did not design us to just fit into one box. You are the sum of many things, including your personality and my 'Assertive Defender' personality will be different to your 'Assertive Defender' personality, although there will be similarities.

Remember you are more than a score or a code! You are made up of many different things and your personality is just one part of you. You will be able to see patterns and themes which help uncover your personality, but don't base everything you know about yourself on responses to questionnaires!

Activity 2: Your Personality

Complete the personality questionnaire on www.16personalities.com

Make a note of the results.

- Were there any surprises?
- Which aspects of your personality profile really resonate with you?
- What does your personality mean for you in terms of your career choices?
- Are there career options you could rule in or out?

Prayer

Father God as I explore my personality,
highlight the things which are important
to You which make me the unique
person You designed.

In Jesus name, Amen.

YOUR DREAMS

*'For God speaks again and again, in dreams,
in visions of the night when deep sleep falls on men
as they lie on their beds. He opens their ears in times like that
and gives them wisdom and instruction'.*

(Job 33:14-16 TLB)

Sometimes God might speak to you in a night-time dream. At other times you might just have dreams about what you would like to do, more like daydreams than dreams you might have when you are asleep. These include dreams about things you always wanted as well as dreams God may have planted in you which are waiting to come to fruition.

There are lots of examples of dreams in the Bible. The most famous are the dreams Joseph had in Genesis 37, which he shared with his father and brothers. 'He said to them, "Listen to this dream I had: We were binding sheaves of grain out in the field when suddenly my sheaf rose and stood upright, while your sheaves gathered around mine and bowed down to it" (Genesis 37:6-7). 'Then he had another dream, and he told it to his brothers. "Listen," he said, "I had another dream, and this time the sun and moon and eleven stars were bowing down to me" (Genesis 37:9).

These dreams were given to Joseph when he was a teenager about to set out on life's journey. They were dreams about his future and took a long time to come to pass. There were many intervening trials and tribulations before they were realised. You can explore more about what happened to Joseph in Chapter Five: EXPERIENCES, but in the meantime, it's safe to say his dreams came true! When there was famine, Joseph's brothers travelled to Egypt, and Joseph remembered his dreams (Genesis 42:9a). The second time they came to Egypt to buy food, his brothers bowed down to him, fulfilling this dream. 'When Joseph came home, they presented to him the gifts they had brought into the house, and they bowed down before him to the ground' (Genesis 43:26).

Although Joseph remembered his dreams when he first received them, he didn't understand what they meant. God used him to interpret the cupbearer's dreams and the baker's dreams in prison. Both these dreams were fulfilled and then Joseph was called to interpret Pharaoh's dreams as well (Genesis 40-41). In the fullness of time, Joseph's dreams became clear and eventually he resettled his entire family and saved many lives due to his excellent stewarding of Egypt's food during the feast years ready for the famine, all foretold by his earlier dreams (Genesis 42-47). I am not suggesting your dreams will be like this, although they may.

Andrea's Dream

A client of mine, Andrea, told me she moved into teaching because of a dream. She had spent more than ten years working in product development and procurement before becoming self-employed. Then 'mid-career' she says,

> *"I was woken up at 6am one morning and God said I was going to be a teacher. It was extraordinary because I had never thought of being a teacher. So, I googled how to train as a teacher and enrolled on a PGCE course.*[7] *At the same time, I saw a large two-page advertorial in a local newspaper about funding for a new inner-city academy and knew I wanted to be a part of it. After completing my teacher training, I spent 10 years working for this city academy, all because of a dream from God".*

Your dreams will be entirely personal to you! You may have shared them with some people, or you may have kept them to yourself. God knows your dreams. You may not have had such explicit dreams as Joseph, but it's likely there were dreams you had as a child which held clues as to God's plan for your career, even if you're not doing exactly what you thought you might be doing in your dreams.

Whilst at university, I had a dream to work in the television industry. This wasn't a literal night-time dream; it was a daydream. More of a musing, an aspiration, a *'wouldn't it be great if I...'* type of daydream. It was a bit of a touch light paper; I would return to this dream and ponder it, despite thinking I would never be 'good enough' or have the ability to work in the television industry. Yet I went on to work for ITV[8] for 10 years. I wasn't a Christian at the time but looking back I can see God's hallmark in it, as a dream He gifted for me to pursue. When I landed a job in television, I had a huge sense of achievement, which you can read more about in Chapter Five: EXPERIENCES.

Michelle's Dreams

Michelle, an actor, comments, *"Looking back at my dreams. I don't remember a time when I didn't want to be an actor."* This was from a very early age and although she wasn't a Christian, she felt a connection with God.

> *"Then the disconnect came, when I was getting older, and questioning things, and more influences were coming in. I still wanted to do acting and drama and English at university, and then when my A levels went all wrong, I was persuaded to do something sensible.*
>
> *So, I did an engineering and business degree instead.*

In retrospect, I don't know how much of this isn't natural bias, because I'm a Christian now, but I feel like the years when I had this dream and was sort of allowing the dream to be free and open and real, about being an actor, were the years I was most closely aligned with God or connected with God. And the years when I tried to do the sensible thing, (not acting) were the years when I was furthest from God."

Sue's Dream

Sue, a doctor, says she wanted to be a PE teacher when she was growing up, so she could be *"outside lots and play lots of sport and encourage others, I thought the PE teacher at school had the best job!"* Sue became a Christian when she was 12 at a Billy Graham crusade[9] at Anfield (Football Stadium in Liverpool) and she says,

"Being an armchair Liverpool supporter, this event was very exciting. I got to step on hallowed turf and I gave my life to Christ.

I was fortunate to go to a Christian school where I was taught a lot about Jesus and given firm foundations. At the age of 14, I was in a geography lesson, and we were learning about India. I can vividly remember thinking, "Oh, I should go and be a missionary." Then I thought, "missionaries aren't very useful. Paul was a tentmaker. I should have a job! What's a useful job? Being a doctor! As I explored this idea I thought actually, this really fits with me, I enjoy chemistry and biology and I find them really interesting. I'm intellectually curious so being a doctor would definitely stretch me and I'd enjoy that. I'd be helping people which was really important to me as well as using the gifts and talents I've been given.

> *So that became my calling. And as I've got older, I've realised you are a missionary wherever you are and whatever job you do, you do not need to go overseas. No matter what job you're doing, you're a missionary. You can stay in the UK and do it.*

Sue's dream to become a PE teacher became a God given dream to become a doctor which she feels fully *"aligned with the personality and gifts God's given me".*

We don't stop dreaming when we reach adulthood! Our dreams continue and can impact all aspects of our lives; it's really exciting when we see them realised.

Has God given you a vivid dream? Write it down. What do you have daydreams about? Keep pondering them. As they continue to rise to the surface in your mind, they are probably worth pursuing, however unrealistic they seem. They will give you clues about your career or the next career steps you will make.

Activity 3: What Dreams has God Given You?

Take a blank piece of paper or open a new Word document.

Answer the questions:

- What do you dream about?
- What things do you daydream about?

(Hint – you might have to go for a walk or take time away from your notebook or computer to really notice what you dream about!)

Write down anything which comes to mind and work quickly.

Then focus on specific areas in your life, including your career and see what comes to mind.

Review the words you have written down and consider adding some more detail.

Ask God to remind you of anything else to add.

Include dreams you had when you were asleep as well as daydreams! Write these down as soon as possible after you wake and include as much detail as you can remember.

Ponder your dreams with God and see what settles.

Don't worry about how realistic you think they are – 'For nothing is impossible with God' (Luke 1:37).

Make a note of these dreams and place them somewhere you can return to time and again.

Prayer

Father God remind me of the dreams for my life and career You have given me. Bring them to mind as I make a note of them now.

In Jesus name, Amen.

YOUR SPIRITUAL GIFTS

'We have different gifts, according to the grace given to each of us'.

(Romans 12:6a)

God gives you spiritual gifts to help the advancement of the Kingdom of God and to be used within the body of Christ. You might ask how these fit within the realm of your career and work life and how they differ from the other gifts God has given you? Spiritual gifts are given from the Holy Spirit to believers and are used for spiritual purposes. Spiritual gifts are gifts of grace[10] which enable God's supernatural power to work through us in ways beyond human possibility.

Spiritual gifts are expressions of God's grace and love exercised through us as His body to fulfil His spiritual purposes. They are generally used for the building up of the body of Christ (believers) and also to bring non-believers into God's Kingdom. God may use a healing or a miracle to draw a non-believer to Himself, or a non-believer may be impacted by the way you have encouraged them or provided hospitality, and this could be a step in their journey to faith.

There are lists of spiritual gifts in the Bible, particularly in: 1 Corinthians 12:7-10 and Romans 12:6-8, as well as evidence of their use in the Old Testament. In the book of Judges, we read of the Spirit of the Lord filling Othniel with power (Judges 3:10); the Spirit of the Lord clothing Gideon with courage and leadership ability (Judges 6:34); and the Spirit of the Lord filling Samson with supernatural strength (Judges 14:6 and Judges 15:14).

Before you begin to explore or review your spiritual gifts, I recommend you pray for discernment, and then take your time! God gives these spiritual gifts, and they can't be boxed up, they can't be compartmentalized in human terms. Identifying spiritual gifts is not an exact science. You can't pick and choose them, but you can ask for them and accept them and then use them in God's service.

Often, spiritual gifts may be given for a season, whereas we mature in others over time. They are like muscles and you need to use them to develop and grow, so it might be you have been given the gift of intercession (praying for other people), but at the moment you are still learning how to do this. Intercession is a spiritual gift God has been growing in me, especially during the lockdown in 2020 as I had more time to intercede. The growth has been gradual and steady. I pray for all my clients, I can't help interceding for them, so I know it's a spiritual gift from God. I long to draw people to God, and I trust God to work beyond my human capabilities for His glory.

As a Christian career coach, I pray for discernment when I'm coaching people, for wisdom so I can understand what a person might not be saying to help me recognise themes and patterns which are important for them. I also use my spiritual gift of encouragement, building people up rather than knocking them down.

In a coaching session with a client, we were discussing the conditions which enable her to thrive in her work. She shared with me her love of the French language and how much she used to enjoy speaking in French, despite not speaking French professionally. I sensed a nudge from the Holy Spirit. This was something important for her and so I probed it gently, trying to encourage her to consider using her expertise in this area, despite her reticence. More than two years later, she told me she was exploring using her

French in a professional capacity and my spirit within me surged with delight. In fact, I felt quite emotional because I knew this was from God and not from me.

In my experience, God doesn't compartmentalise our work and personal lives. I am equally called to intercede for people in my life regardless of whether they are my clients or not. I know when I bring people before God in prayer, He hears my prayers and responds to them. Things are opened in the heavenly realms which will make a difference in people's lives.

Sheralyn's Spiritual Gifts

I interviewed Sheralyn, lawyer and entrepreneur, about her spiritual gifts and how she uses them in her career. There were some spiritual gifts which immediately resonated with her including Administration, Apostleship, Encouragement, Faith, Hospitality, Leadership, Mercy, Tongues, Knowledge and Wisdom. She could speak easily about these things.

> "**Administration** - *If you read the description of administration it's a 'Yes', though if you looked at my desk, I'd say 'No' because it's a mess, but I do actually fit quite well into 'Administration' because I do strategies, planning, goal setting and I enjoy doing those things. And, I usually have a plan."*
>
> **Faith** – *Yes, absolutely. I step out in faith all the time.* **Hospitality** – *Yes, a big fat Yes.* **Knowledge** – *Yes, definitely and the more my knowledge of the Bible grows. This goes along with* **Wisdom** *really. Somebody prophesied over me that I was going to want to study wisdom, and I've done lots of studies on Proverbs, and I*

can draw conclusions quickly and draw upon sections of the of Old Testament when I'm talking to people, which I didn't used to be able to do in the past. **Leadership** - *Yes.* **Tongues** – *yes, I can speak in tongues".*

There were several gifts which Sheralyn indicated a 'maybe'.

"**Evangelism** – *maybe - this surprised me, because I do a lot of evangelism, but I don't particularly seek opportunities for this; it's not something I strive to do. I do it all the time, but it's through training rather than a passion to do it in the first place.* **Giving** - *maybe. I always give lots of time and lots of money but I'm not sure I can do it cheerfully all the time. I still do it because I'm obedient, but I wouldn't say it's a gift.* **Healing** – *maybe. I have seen healing. I've prayed for healing. I remember the first time I prayed for a lady who had a frozen shoulder in Africa. She could barely lift it. I prayed for her and felt heat in the palms of my hands as the healing happened. Does that mean I've got the gift, or does it mean I'm learning to use this gift?* **Service** – *maybe. I like serving. I see opportunities, but generally I'm not so much in the background. I'm usually up front and centre. Perhaps that's the Leadership gifting seen as servant leadership. You wouldn't find me on the the overhead projector unless they were desperate!"*

Interestingly, many of these are activities we are all called to do as Christians, even if we don't feel specifically spiritually gifted in these areas. And as Sheralyn comments, we do them out of obedience and because we are part of the Church.

I asked Sheralyn how these spiritual gifts were apparent in her career.

"Firstly, as a lawyer, it's very much pastoral, helping, serving, those kinds of things. Discerning whether or not to pray for a client's bad back, for example. But I do share my faith and discern how much to talk about it. Sometimes when I'm doing a complex probate, I meet with clients several times and as I get to know them, I can share my faith journey captured in 'Couch to Kilimanjaro' (the book Sheralyn has written). This resonates with clients because my own faith journey, returning to Jesus, came after my parents died so there is a connection with the probate clients who are dealing with their parents' deaths. I've been able to share how Jesus has got me to where I am now. God gives me the knowledge and the wisdom to be able to give them the right answers, legally and spiritually, and I can be very confident in what I'm doing."

Sherlyn has set up a social enterprise called Woofterful® Doggy Daycare. This aims to provide dog owners somewhere safe and secure with high quality care in a nurturing and truly dog focused environment, whilst also supporting survivors of modern-day slavery who will be trained to provide this care. She says,

"Well, it's total faith. Faith with a capital F because I've never done it before. I'm no expert but I am becoming one! I'm part way through my qualification in doggy daycare so I can get the licence. I'm really listening to God. There's a problem with objections to the planning application for the centre, and I'm not worried because I know God will sort it out! He's already connected me with a Planning Consultant, who is not a Christian, but has held my hand through the process, and loves the vision, and he's provided the right advice and guidance every step of the way.

God even gave me the name! I was driving back from my then work on my way to collect my own dog from doggie daycare when I thought "If I'm going to do this, God, you've got to give me a good name and "Woofterful®" came straight to mind. As soon as I arrived home I Google searched the trademark as well as searching Companies House for the name. I'm a lawyer after all. I realised 'it's a new word, it doesn't exist'. So, I applied for the trademark straightaway, and I was awarded it within three months. The guy who dealt with it said it was the easiest trademark decision he ever had to make. Wow! So, it was an obvious word from God for me."

Now, it's time to identify your spiritual gifts.

I have created a checklist to help you start to identify or review your own spiritual gifts which you can find in Appendix One. As you work through this checklist, I recommend asking Christian friends, colleagues and pastors for their views on what spiritual gifts they think God has given you and why they think you might have these spiritual gifts.

I would urge some caution in this area because none can know the mind of God (1 Corinthians 2:16) and exactly how He wants to move in your life. This is about being open to the spiritual gifts God wants to give you and being open to how He wants to use them in your career.

Activity 4:
Your Spiritual Gifts

Prayerfully complete the Spiritual Gifts Checklist in Appendix One.

Make a note of your spiritual gifts.

Administration	Apostleship
Craftsmanship	Creative Communication
Discernment	Encouragement
Evangelism	Faith
Giving	Healing
Helps	Hospitality
Interpretation of Tongues	Intercession
Knowledge	Leadership
Mercy	Miracles
Pastor/Shepherd	Prophecy
Service	Teaching
Tongues	Wisdom

- How do you use these in your career? Write down some specific examples.
- Ask Christian friends, colleagues and pastors how they have seen you use your spiritual gifts.
- What evidence do they have to suggest a particular gift is true for you?

Prayer

Father God thank You for the gifts of
Your Holy Spirit, as I pray through
the checklist quicken my heart for
the spiritual gifts which are relevant to me.

In Jesus name, Amen

REFLECTION ACTIVITY: YOUR UNIQUE GIFTS

God has gifted you with a unique set of personal gifts which you have unwrapped in this chapter. Take a moment to review them and reflect on what you have been given.

Your Natural Gifts

- What really resonated with you as you reflected on the things you did as a child?
- Make a note of the natural gifts God has given you, the things which come easily to you, and you feel you don't have to try when you are doing this or behaving in a particular way.

Your Personality

- How would you describe your personality using one sentence?
- Was there anything which surprised you about your personality?
- Was there something that really made sense to you which might impact your career or choice of career?

Your Dreams

- In a sentence or two write down your dreams... what if I could ...?

Your Spiritual Gifts

- Make a note of your main spiritual gifts.
- Consider how you might use these gifts in your career.

Prayer

Father God, thank you for my natural gifts,
my personality, my dreams and the
spiritual gifts You have given me.
Help me to use all these for your glory.

In Jesus name, Amen.

GRACE

Gifts

Relationships

Abilities

Curiosities

Experiences

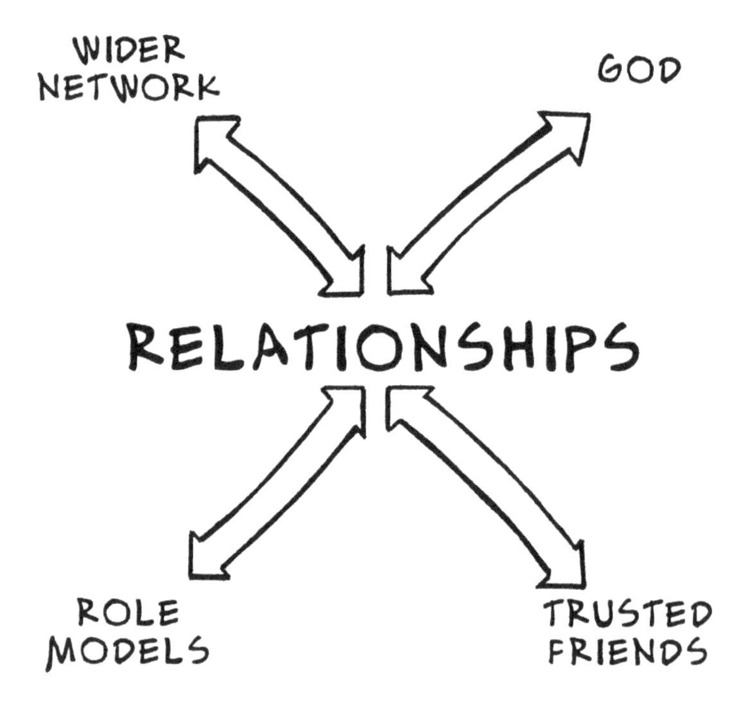
WIDER NETWORK
GOD
RELATIONSHIPS
ROLE MODELS
TRUSTED FRIENDS

Chapter Two: RELATIONSHIPS

'I will be a Father to you, and you will be my sons and daughters, says the Lord Almighty'.

(2 Corinthians 6:18)

God Himself exists in loving community in the Trinity, one God in three persons, Father, Son and Holy Spirit. Since we are made in His image (Genesis 1:27), we too are designed to live in loving community with others, as well as with God as He invites us to join in His loving community, as His adopted sons and daughters (Ephesians 1:5).

We are relational beings, and our relationships with other people are essential to our overall wellbeing and sense of purpose. We are connected to many people, some more closely than others, some remotely via social media, and some we see regularly in person.

Dr. Dave Smith's book, *God's Plan for Your Wellbeing,* suggests our vertical relationship with God and our horizontal relationship with other people are essential to our wellbeing. He writes, 'Made in His image (see Genesis 1:27), we are designed to live in community, loving and caring for one another. This means that while we have 'vertical' needs that can only be satisfied by a close, personal relationship with God Himself, we also have 'horizontal' needs that can only be met by healthy relationships with other people'.[1]

Your relationships are essential for your career journey, and this chapter will help you explore those relationships, starting with God. He has a plan for your career, which He will reveal throughout your life, so it makes sense to cultivate **Your Relationship with God** to find out what He has to say about how you should spend your working life.

God also puts people in our lives as **Trusted Friends**, the people we are close to and feel able to share our career aspirations and dreams with. Jesus chose 12 people to be His disciples, and three of these people He was particularly close to, His close confidants. These people are essential to our careers as people who know us really well and can provide trusted advice and guidance.

Beyond this is your **Wider Network**; the surprising number of people you actually know, all of whom can help in your career, and you can help as well. Then there are Christian **Role Models** you can learn from, those you know personally, and those in the public eye, or people who have gone before us who can teach us so much from their example.

At the end of this chapter you can take some time to gather your relationships into one place, in circles of relationship and as you read this chapter ask God to clarify your important relationships, recognising they are essential for your career, wellbeing and sense of purpose.

Prayer

Father God thank You for inviting me
into a relationship with You.
Thank You for all the significant people
You have connected me to.
Thank You for the wider connections
You have given me and also for the
Christians who have gone ahead of me
who I can draw inspiration from.

In Jesus name, Amen

YOUR RELATIONSHIP WITH GOD

'You hem me in, behind and before,
and You lay Your hand upon me'.
(Psalm 139:5)

I have discovered God always goes before me. It's like the pillar of cloud and pillar of fire that led the Israelites through the desert in Exodus 13:21. His provision is always a step ahead of me. When I look back, I see his hand on me as well. This has been as true for my career as in any other aspects of my life. Even in the difficult times when I coudn't see the way ahead, when a job offer didn't pan out or my freelance work dried up, God was still with me and He still had a plan, even if I didn't know what it was. He has been utterly faithful even when I have not, loving me through my failures and mistakes and always drawing me back into His loving arms.

Consider the story of the Prodigal Son (Luke 15:11-32) I told in the INTRODUCTION. This story illustrates how much God loves us. It's a wonderful story of repentance, forgiveness and redemption, demonstrating God's amazing grace. When the lost son recognises he has gone astray and would be better off at home as a hired hand, he sets off to return having no idea his father is waiting, watching and longing for him. 'But while he was still a long way off, his father saw him and was filled with compassion for him; he ran to his son, threw his arms around him and kissed him' (Luke 15:20).

Many of us reading these words can't fail to be moved by the response the son received from the father, but we don't always realise this is the response God has for us, too. We are stuck in a mentality believing God is a hard task master and believe, like the Prodigal Son, God wants us to be a hired hand, because we have sinned and are not worthy. The son himself believed this as he says, "I am no longer worthy to be called your son; make me like one of your hired men" (Luke 15:19).

Imagine his delight at the ecstatic greeting and full restoration he received. This is the greeting and restoration we have from God as well because of Jesus. It could be you've heard, *'God has adopted you as His son or daughter'*, but it's just head knowledge. This was the case for me. I had to turn away from past experiences which held me bound, feeling rejected and unloved, I repented and journeyed back to God. I found out God was watching and waiting for me and this deepened my understanding of my relationship with Him.

We are not told how long the son's return journey was, but elsewhere in the Bible, 40 days seems to be a good yardstick as a time frame for returning to God. This is how long it took me, to begin to lay down my brokenness and sense of being unworthy, through reading specific Bible verses relevant to me, and through prayer, renouncing lies which bound me and affirming instead the truths God thinks about me. By the end of the 40 days, I really knew I was a Child of God. Amazing! I was free from the sense of rejection and unworthiness which had held me captive and free to love Father God as His child.[2]

I definitely had 'head knowledge'; I was a Child of God, but I'm not sure it had fully penetrated my heart. A few years later I attended a Christian Women's Weekend Away, where we explored the truth of our identity. We were asked to consider our identity, and to search the Psalms to see what God was saying to us. I glibly thought, *"I know who I am – I'm a Child of God"* – job done!

The weekend was being led by Ruth Rice, Director of Renew Wellbeing and she told her own story of brokenness and restoration. One of the stories she told really resonated with me. You can read this in her book *Slow Down Show Up and Pray*. She asked us, *"Where are you sitting?"* When she asked God this question about herself, God led her to the story of Deborah in Judges 4, and she saw herself sitting between Ramah the place of weeping and Bethel the place of God.[3]

'Deborah, a prophetess, the wife of Lappidoth, was leading Israel at the time. She held court under the Palm of Deborah between Ramah and Bethel in the hill country of Ephraim, and the Israelites came to her to have their disputes decided' (Judges 4:4-5).

As Ruth described how God had used this story to help her see how God shows His love to His people, she asked us where we thought we were sitting? Reflecting on her talk that evening, I asked God where I was sitting. I knew I wasn't sitting under the Palm of Deborah so where was I sitting? As I pondered this with God, He revealed that I wasn't sitting in a great place! I realised I was like Jonah, sitting on the east side of the city of Nineveh under a shelter he had built, feeling resentful and disheartened because God showed compassion on the sinful people of Nineveh (Jonah 4:1-11).

I have to say I was a bit shocked! Jonah was a reluctant prophet, who ran away from God's command to preach to the people of Nineveh, got swallowed by a big whale during a storm, before he came to his senses and preached to the people of Nineveh. The people repented and returned to God, but Jonah was frustrated and angry because God had compassion on these corrupt and debauched people, so he went off to sulk (Jonah 1-4).

Oh dear! That's where I was sitting; sulking, resentful and reluctant. It didn't feel like a great place to be, and certainly not a great place from which to help other people. I wondered how long I would stay there, or when I could get up. I really wasn't sure how I was going to move from that desolate place.

As the weekend went on, we were asked to consider what we were carrying. What was in the metaphorical rucksack I was carting around with me? Actually, at this point I felt I was leaning on my rucksack under the withered vine, feeling pretty resentful and miserable. Ruth went on to talk about where Jesus is sitting, and I realised it wasn't about where I was sitting, it was about where Jesus is sitting in the heavenly realms, which makes the difference. As Paul writes in Ephesians 2:6, '... God raised us up with Christ and seated us *with Him* (my italics) in the heavenly realms in Christ Jesus'. Jesus is sitting in the heavenly realms and I was sitting there with Him. In fact, as Christians, we have all been raised with Christ and sit with Him in the heavenly realms.

Oh Wow! Jesus is sitting in the heavenly realms and I am sitting there with Him. I'm no longer sitting with Jonah under the withered tree, I'm sitting with Jesus. How awesome! In that moment I understood what mattered: where Jesus was sitting not where I was sitting. God was drawing me back to Him. I repented of my reluctance and when the time came to go forward for prayer I obeyed. A lady I didn't know prayed for me, laying her hands on my shoulders, and God spoke through her. This is what He said to me.

"You are my beloved Daughter,
and I am your Father.
I smiled when you were born
I smiled when you were born again
I smiled when you came forward today!"

I was blown away! I am not just a Child of God; I am His beloved Daughter! The knowledge of my identity and relationship with Him had moved from my head to my heart. Despite my reluctance and resentfulness, He chose to speak to me out of His deep compassion, to affirm His love for me as 'beloved' and to make the relationship deeply personal. I am His beloved Daughter.

You too are God's beloved Son or Daughter. It's from this place of deep love, acceptance and security that our love for God can flow more freely; from a place of joy rather than duty; a place of ease rather than striving; a place of familial relationship rather than hired hand.

Do you want to know God's will and provision for your career? Take the time to get to know Him well and grow your relationship with Him. I imagine the Prodigal Son wanting to hear all about the plans his father has and how he can work alongside him in restored relationship, relieved and excited to be home.

Mark's Relationship with God

I interviewed Mark, Director of *Status Social*, to find out how his relationship with Jesus has impacted his career. His relationship with God has been vibrant and very experienced based. He says,

> *"From the start, my relationship with God has been a personal one based on my individual encounters with him, rather than through the Church, or Bible reading or even interaction with other Christians, although they have all played a part. For me it's about being excited and enthusiastic and feeling it's very much a living relationship.*

I was baptised in the Holy Spirit in the middle of a pub in Hull even though I had no idea who the Holy Spirit was. I was given the spiritual gift of tongues without knowing it was a spiritual language and I thought, "What on earth is this?" When Jesus first healed somebody through me, I was in Church and felt an overwhelming desire to pray for the person next to me who had an injury from a fairground accident, and she was healed. I was responding to the Holy Spirit prompting me, despite not understanding what was happening. So, my relationship with God is very much about Him showing me things and speaking to me and hearing His voice. It's dynamic."

Mark says there have been real ups and downs in his career and for a lot of the time his career and faith were separate.

"I struggled to marry the two. I was a journalist for 20 years and being a journalist and a Christian was really hard. Working on a daily newspaper, I'd be sent to interview people where somebody had just died, and I'd have to be intrusive to get their story. Or I'd be sent to knock on the doors of people who I knew didn't want to be talked to. I'd go to murders and car crashes, and report on things that were often really tough.

There were times when my faith did come through, when I responded in the right way as a Christian. If I knew something was wrong, and I didn't want to do it morally, I would take a stand. Although my colleagues would have known I was a Christian, they certainly wouldn't have thought that I acted particularly like a Christian. I didn't speak about being Christian or about knowing Jesus in the passionate way I do now. I think having your own business gives you freedom to be able to speak openly about Jesus."

Mark shared some stories about how God directed his career.

"I was working for Pizza Hut, because I'd lost my job in a newspaper, wondering how I would get back into journalism. One night, driving down the motorway to a party in Hull, God said to me, "Tonight I'm going to get you back into journalism." I thought, "Okay, but is this thought from me or is it God?" When I arrived at the party, I went to get a drink and a guy I didn't know stood next to me. He asked what I did, and when I told him I was a journalist, he replied, "I'm a journalist too! I work for the Yorkshire Post. We really need journalists like you in Grimsby. You should go and set up a Press Agency". So, that's what I did. I set up a Press Agency. I was back in journalism again, on the back of a conversation with the first person I met at that party.

Another time, I decided to fast and pray for God to show me what He wanted me to do next. As I was praying the phone rang. It was my friend who said that there was a job available at Premier Christian Radio. He said, "You should apply for it." I thought, "Wow, this is God's answer. I'm going to be a radio journalist." I applied for the job, but their response was that I was too inexperienced to move into radio. I thought, "Oh, I don't understand, I'm sure God was speaking to me about becoming a radio journalist". About six months later I had set up the Press Agency and I was supplying newspaper stories to a local radio station in Hull. They rang me up and said, "Mark, we want you to apply for one of our jobs", despite my lack of radio experience. And so, I moved into radio! Going from newspapers to radio was a bit of a jump, especially in commercial radio. It was really unexpected, but I know God steered me to this in my career. I think the more confident you are in your relationship with Jesus, the more you care about God than your career, the more your career will blossom because you're dealing with God rather than doing it for yourself. There is a point where I think if you put God first, and you recognise that He is more important than everything else, there's a good chance that your career and your faith will merge into one and it'll become something much more powerful."

Just as Mark has learned to recognise God's voice, as you spend time with God you too can learn to recognise His voice. Jesus says, "My sheep listen to my voice; I know them, and they follow me" (John 10:27). God is not in a hurry, and so in order to hear Him it helps to slow down and take time to hear what He has to say. Find a time and space that suits you best, either a quiet spot at home, or on a daily walk. Take time to ponder with God, ask Him questions and see what comes to mind. You may need to jot your thoughts down when you get back from a walk. Or if you prefer, sit quietly with Him. You could play some worship music and get out your Bible and journal.

I have tried both these options. I really value scheduled time to sit and pray. I use a structured approach which includes worship, generally listening to songs but sometimes I sing too, before reading a passage from the Bible and meditating on it, writing down anything I feel prompted to note. Then I write out my prayers in longhand. God often uses this time to 'speak' to me through Bible verses which seem particularly apt, or through the way I am prompted to pray. You can read more about one of His answers to my prayers in Chapter Four: CURIOSITIES - Your Revelations.

I have also gone on walks with God, usually taking my dog as well! I find this time of unstructured prayer becomes a time of musing and pondering with God just enjoying His presence and being with Him. Sometimes He has used these prayer walks to speak to me. There was one time I went on a prayer walk with God and I was particularly upset because I had stepped out and applied for a part time job which I felt God wanted me to do. I was invited to interview and had a great time with the interviewers and left the room buzzing, but I was not selected for the job. I was upset and confused, had I misheard God? So, I went on a walk and poured out my heart. He didn't speak to me in words, but I did gain a sense of peace that even though I hadn't got the job, I had done as God had wanted and applied for it. The rational part of me knew the interviewers had selected the right person for the job, because they would have prayed and I knew the person they chose was a better skills-fit than I was, but at the time it was very painful.

My prayers about becoming a career coach were a mix of sitting down with God and my notebook plus going on walks. God didn't necessarily speak to me with words but with heart-felt impressions and a sense of profound peace. Confirmation God is speaking to you can come from a circumstance, something happens that confirms what you feel God impressing on you. Or it could be a Scripture passage which really resonates with your heart. God might speak to you in an audible voice, or a voice you hear in your heart. It could be someone else says something to you that connects with what you think God is saying. Think of this as a Godly conversation. He will connect with you in ways which are unique to how He made you.

Lisa's Relationship with God

If you're not sure about what God is saying about your career, why not slow down and ask Him over a period of time… this is what Lisa, Head of Operations for *Isaiah 61M* did. I interviewed her about her career change, and she said,

> *"First of all, it's about making time to pray, to have a conversation with God. It's not all about asking God for what He can do for you, it's about giving thanks, and I give thanks every day, because I just feel so blessed. We have to count our blessings. We are so fortunate for all kinds of reasons. I like to pray when I'm outside, I love to pray when I'm in nature and I'm walking, I just feel closer to God, and I feel I can focus more and engage more. And the praying becomes sort of talking about, "Well, I think this is what you want me to do."*
>
> *Then it's not just the conversations, the prayer, the feeling on the heart from God, it's the actual physical experiences which occur, which make you think you are where you are meant to be going. This is when the thoughts and impressions you have are backed up by happenings in real life, and it just cements the feeling you get from God."*

As I mentioned earlier, 40 days is a significant time frame in the Bible. In the Old Testament it rained for 40 days whilst Noah sheltered in the ark (Genesis 7:17); Moses went up Mount Sinai for 40 days to meet with God (Exodus 24:18); Jesus spent 40 days fasting after his baptism (Matthew 4:2, Mark 1:13, Luke 4:2); and there were 40 days between His resurrection and ascension when the disciples waited for Jesus (Acts 1:3).

Do you want to hear from God about your career?

I suggest you set aside 40 days to spend time with Him in prayer. This is about trusting God. 'Trust God from the bottom of your heart; don't try to figure out everything on your own. Listen for God's voice in everything you do, everywhere you go; He's the one who will keep you on track' (Proverbs 3:5-6 MSG).

Michelle's Relationship with God

I interviewed Michelle, about her 40 days of prayer for her career. She said, *"This verse about trusting God really summed up my experience."* By praying daily for her career, she found she was open to hear God in *"all sorts of unexpected ways,"* including through inspirational cards from Christian Aid which resonated with her, listening to podcasts of interviews with industry professionals as well as scriptures from the Bible. Her process included a simple prayer,

> *"Dear Heavenly Father, I know You love me, You have plans to give me hope and a future and absolutely nothing can separate me from Your love. Please, I pray guide me in my career, give me clarity and help me follow the path You have set down for me, in Jesus name, Amen."*

She *"literally ticked off the days"* as she prayed this for 40 days, alongside reading some scripture verses which she felt were significant to her as well as keeping a journal of her experience.

As an actor, Michelle's work is sporadic and so she also works within the community, where she lives. During the 40 days, God seemed to speak into all these work areas not just her acting.

When I spoke with Michelle, she explained,

> *"I had a sense of peace in my heart at the end of the 40 days, especially about two actions I felt prompted to take; one stepping up into a new post; and the other walking away from my agent. From the prayers, I had the courage to trust God without being clear about the outcome. Then a third opportunity arose for some part time work which fits me in my best way of being, suits me really well and I feel like God has given me those openings.*
>
> *During the 40 days of praying, I also encountered a difficult experience with a co-worker. Instead of reacting in a way I might have reacted in the past, I discovered through prayer a really clear process for dealing with this. I can take this God inspired process with me forever.*
>
> *God also released me from my doubts about my career as an actor, and whether this was in line with His plan for my life. As I prayed about this, I felt God had put this desire in my heart, and He is opening up avenues for acting, as it says in the Bible, 'Delight in the Lord and He will give you the desires of your heart' (Psalm 37:4). I think it's about trusting the process. We always want to get to journey's end but actually, the learning comes throughout the journey."*

It was really encouraging to hear Michelle's experience with prayer, and as you've read mine and Lisa's as well, you will see this is a gentle grace filled process, not something you have to strive at. When you look back at the end of 40 days, you'll be able to see where and how God is at work in your career and how your relationship with Him has deepened as you spend more time with Him.

Often, we are so busy presenting our requests to God we forget to wait for an answer. There are times when we have to wait longer than we would like for God's answer, so don't be surprised when this happens to you. Just wait! Daniel had to wait 21 days for God to answer his prayer (Daniel 10:13). Sometimes God waits the full 40 days before answering.

Activity 5: 40 Days of Prayer for Your Career

Take time to ponder with God.

Choose one Bible passage and one or two specific verses which resonate with you.

Write them down so you can read them each day.

Here are some Bible passages you could consider -

- Parable of the Talents – Matthew 25:14-30
- The Wife of Noble Character – Proverbs 31:10-31
- The Vine and The Branches – John 15:1-17
- A Letter to the Exiles - Jeremiah 29:1-14

And some specific verses:–

Jeremiah 29:11	Proverbs 3:5-6	Psalm 32:8
Proverbs 16:3	Psalm 37:4	James 1:17
Psalm 127:1	Romans 8:28	Matthew 6:33
Matthew 6:34	Matthew 7:7	James 1:5
Proverbs 20:5	Ephesians 2:10	Psalm 139:16b

Then ask Him a question and wait for His answer!

Let the questions rest in your heart whilst you write them down. As things come to mind which you think might be from God jot them down and ask for confirmation.

When you've heard from God, pray for peace.

Remember to count off 40 days, so you know where you are, and if you miss a day or two just pick up where you left off!

Prayer

Father God – I long to know You more and
I pledge to spend more time with You, through
Your word and in prayer, to get to know You
and understand the things which are important
to You. Father God thank You for sending Jesus
and the Holy Spirit – search me and
know me as I long to know You.

In Jesus name, Amen.

YOUR TRUSTED FRIENDS

'Plans fail for lack of counsel,
but with many advisors they succeed'.
(Proverbs 15:22)

There have been times in my career when I've been tempted to 'go it alone' especially as a freelancer when working on my own became the norm. However, I found I then became isolated and stifled. I realised I need other people to share ideas with, to hear wise counsel, to spark creativity, to grow as a person, to have fun.

Jesus didn't work alone. He had 12 disciples, and several women, including Mary Magdalene, Joanna, and Suzanna 'supporting Him out of their own means' (Luke 8:1-3). He was friends with Lazarus, Martha and Mary (Luke 10:38-41). The gospels record many of the conversations and interactions He had with these people, as He shared His wisdom with them.

Although Jesus had 12 disciples, there were three who were particularly close to Him; Peter, John and James who were with Him for His transfiguration (Matthew 17:1) and also in the Garden of Gethsemane (Matthew 26:37). These were the three people most close to Him who He confided in, who He felt deeply about as His closest friends.

Through the years, I've prayed with other people about my career, three of us in a prayer triplet, and in larger groups in home group settings. I've sought counsel from these people, seeking discernment if I feel God is leading me in a particular direction.

The small prayer triplet is particularly helpful because I can be totally honest about my fears and worries as well as being open to their counsel, because I know they will be listening to God too. Jesus tells us, "For where two or three gather in my name, there am I with them" (Matthew 18:20).

Sue's Trusted Friends

I asked Sue, what difference she felt being in a prayer triplet made to her career,

> *"I think it's a really safe space, where I can say anything, and I know it won't be repeated. I can be me. And I will be loved and supported but I will also be challenged, so there's accountability there as well. It's not just earthly wisdom but knowing friends are praying and listening for God's voice for me, especially when you're in the thick of things and can't always hear God's voice clearly for yourself.*
>
> *I've gone through some very difficult decisions in my career, about what work to take on or which direction to go in or when I've been considering different options or doors have closed on something I wanted. I've been able to be at peace about those experiences rather than angry because I've known my prayer triplet have prayed for me and with me and I've been able to hold decisions lightly and leave them with God. Having these people listening to God and giving me Christian counsel has been invaluable."*

If you would like to start a prayer triplet, there are some great resources about setting up fellowship bands at www.inspiremovement.org.[4]

As well as my prayer triplet, there are other people I consider close friends, just as the other nine disciples were close to Jesus. These are the people in your life who will give you inspiration and support and can help you make decisions about your career. They may not all be Christians, but they will be people who know you well. God is not limited to speaking into our lives and careers only through Christians. These are the people you can turn to for advice, and the people you celebrate with in good times. I encourage you to be clear about who these people are and to pray for them and meet with them regularly.

You are not meant to search for God's purpose for your career in isolation. So, it's really important to establish who these important people will be. This shouldn't take too much thought! You will already know who these people are. They are the people you can share your career ideas and considerations with. People who know you well and who you can trust, who encourage and champion you, who help fill you with confidence, who you feel really at ease speaking to. You don't need an invitation to speak with them; there's no agenda, the relationship is natural and there is support and encouragement from people who have your best interests at heart.

These relationships are two-way, give and take, so there are times when they will be supporting you in your career and times when you will be supporting them. Just as an aside, it's highly likely you won't just discuss your careers with these people. Of course, you'll be discussing lots of other areas of your life with them as well!

Activity 6:
Your Career Champions

Take a moment to consider your close relationships, your trusted friends.

- Who are these people?
- Write down their names.
- Pray for each of them by name.
- Reflect on how often you speak with them – do you need to speak with them more often?
- Give thanks for them and ask God that they might speak into your life about your career.

Prayer

Father God – bring to mind the people who
should be in my inner circle, my career
champions, the people who know me well.
Thank You for these friendships and help
me to be open to anything You want to
say through them about my career.
Help me to weigh their words carefully
and to seek Your confirmation of them.

In Jesus name, Amen.

YOUR WIDER NETWORK

'Without good direction, people lose their way; the more wise counsel you follow, the better your chances'.

(Proverbs 11:14 MSG)

At the beginning of the letters Paul wrote in the New Testament, you will see he states who he is, followed by a list of people he is writing to, believers, saints, the Church, followed by blessing them with God's grace and peace. Each letter starts this way. Often, they end with a message of love and grace as well.

Paul knew a lot of people through his travels as an itinerant preacher and missionary. In Romans 16, Paul sends greetings to at least 27 people, and their wider networks or Churches. He also mentions another eight people who join him in sending greetings. This network was essential to the building of the early Church and to support Paul.

In the same way, your network is an important element in your career, the people you know and connect with, who in turn connect you with other people. A lot of people shy away from networking but in fact it's really just about relationships and getting to know people.

The world of social media makes this so easy. At the click of a button, you can connect or reconnect with people to keep in touch. However, building good relationships is important and this can take time and requires a bit more than just a click of a button. It's not about what you can get out of a relationship, it's about building up those relationships, so they become two-way, spending time getting to know people. When these relationships are in place, then God can use them to communicate with you about your career and make connections which can result in career moves and job changes.

God has really used my network in developing my career. As a consultant it was my contacts, and the associates I worked with, who gave me work or referred me, or alerted me to work opportunities. The husband of one of my trusted friends recommended me for a role I interviewed for and subsequently got. As a career coach God has grown my network, through the people I met when I was becoming accredited, to the people I have met since, all in answer to prayer.

During the Covid-19 pandemic I realised I needed to spend more time on social media networking. When I set up Conley Career Coaching, I thought I would be spending time having coffee with people in coffee shops and going to physical networking meetings. Obviously with lockdown this didn't happen. My somewhat unformed prayer was, *"Father God I need some help, I can't do this on my own!"* Into my head popped the name of someone I had encountered at a Christians In Business conference I had attended before lockdown. I got in touch with him, and he connected me to a Kingdom Business Network, which is a group of business people who meet once a week to share business insights and pray for each other. This has been such a tremendous blessing and has connected me to a wide range of people. Just by showing up at the networking meeting each week on Zoom® I have got to know them, and they have got to know me. Through this network, I also met Ladey Adey who has mentored me through the exciting journey of writing this career book.

Ladey's Expert Thoughts on Your Wider Network

Ladey Adey is an authority on networking so I asked her how her career had benefited from her wider network. She says,

"Everything, for me begins with God. God being not one person, but three. So, it's my relationship with God the Father, God the Son, and God the Holy Spirit. They come with me when I do any networking. This enables me to hear His quiet still voice when I meet people to know whether I should trust them, whether I like them and whether I want to carry on and do work or business with them. So this is where I start.

As a Christian, meeting people in person, I never believed it was luck when I sat next to a particular person, or I met a particular person and hit it off. I see these as 'Godinstances' and you meet people He plans for you to meet!

As a Royal Air Force family, every time we moved place I lost my old networks, and had to begin new ones. This could be simply meeting people such as a next-door neighbour and saying, which doctor do you use, which dentist do you use? What is the school like around here? Which hairdresser do you use? These become your natural network, built around how you want to live your life.

From there, your wider network includes whatever interests you have, crafts or sports, with golf as a huge networking opportunity for personal and business contacts. Your network includes the church you attend.

The most important aspect of your wider network is the relationships you develop and cultivate, through

getting to know people personally. This is the same in both a personal and work setting. When I worked in the Charitable Sector, as a regional manager, I knew I wanted to create a network within the profession and within my company. Whenever I went to the HQ in London, I would ensure to 'walk the floor' to meet people in finance, marketing and all departments so people could put my face to my name and know which region I represented. They could get to know me. This became my professional network. Over time, I grew my network beyond the company to people in the same profession but working for other organisations and so my network became even wider.

When networking, I'm always looking for the synergy. What have I got to offer that might help this person, either now or in the future? I also like to collect details so I can follow up in the future, and although this requires patience, I like to keep in the long game. To me, business networking is just an extended Christmas card list. As you send a Christmas card out every year, you have to at least put one thing out to each person and keep in touch with them!

Recently, my career has been hugely impacted by my wider network when I started my own business. Zoom® became the predominant way of networking groups meeting. I wrote a book, 'Successful Business Networking Online', and my business quadrupled overnight because I could reach more people unlike when you're meeting in person and you've only got your geographical base. Networking has been essential to the growth of my business and career."

Who do you know and where do they work?

Most of us know a lot more people than we realise. Just have a think about who you know from Church, the school gate, your friendship group, societies or clubs you're involved in, your neighbours, any networking groups you belong to. When on Facebook, review your 'Friends' and reach out to people who you sense God prompting you to. When on Instagram, regularly keep up to date with your contacts. Remember, for career purposes, networking is about building relationships and as Ladey suggests you should be reaching out to each person to keep in touch with them.

Then, consider people you know through your work. LinkedIn, the predominant global professional networking platform, is a great place to start. Review your connections and consider how up to date they are. How well do you know your professional connections? How about Twitter? Who could you follow and tweet with? Try not to be overwhelmed by volume. This is about quality connections, people you know personally, rather than mere acquaintances.

As you progress through your career journey, who is God connecting you with?

Activity 7:
Who is in Your Wider Network?

I recommend grabbing a large piece of paper to create a spidergram of people you know.

Fill it with headings such as work, school, church, clubs, friendships and so on and then list the names of the people you know under this.

Try to do this fairly quickly and write down any names that come to mind, you could use different colours to distinguish between different groups.

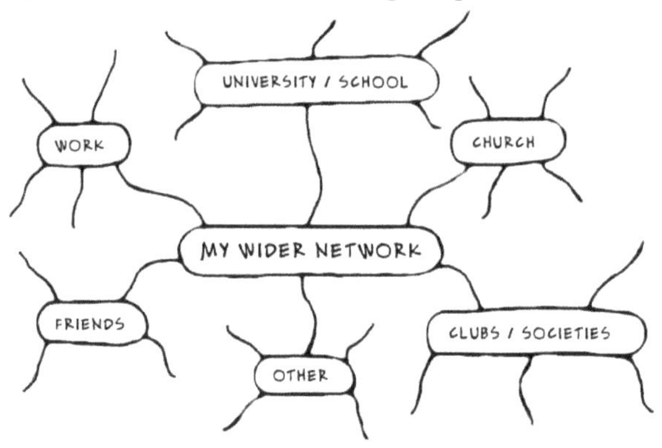

Consider who you know on Facebook, Instagram and other social networks. Scroll through prayerfully otherwise your spidergram might grow extra legs!

Then go back through the names and jot down the work these people do or their job title if you know it.

Review your network on LinkedIn.

- How up to date is it?
- Do you need to cull some contacts?
- Who would you like to connect with professionally?

Review your Twitter account.

- Who could you follow and tweet with?

Put a † next to people who you know are Christians. God can use anyone to help you explore career options, but with Christians there is an added 'God dimension' to the relationship.

Keep your spidergram somewhere safe so you can refer back to it when you are searching for your next job.

Prayer

Father God – help me to be aware of the people
You are drawing into my wider network,
to pay attention to what they say and do,
and to ponder this alongside all the
other information I am receiving.
I pray You would make it abundantly clear
what is from You and what is not.

In Jesus name, Amen.

YOUR ROLE MODELS

'Instruct the wise and they will be wiser still; teach the righteous and they will add to their learning'.

(Proverbs 9:9)

As well as your wider network you may have people who act as role models for you. These could be people you know from a work setting, from whom you can learn. They might be a manager, or supervisor, or they could be someone who works in a similar industry or sector to you but not actually with you, or people you aspire to be like. A role model is someone who inspires you so much you want to emulate their achievements.

I'm not talking about celebrity role models, I'm talking about the people who impress you by the work they do, or the people you admire because of the way they behave in their career. My first boss was a tremendous role model for me. He knew how to encourage me, he knew how to delegate, he knew how to share his vision and he was clear about what he expected of me. I learnt a huge amount from him which has benefited me greatly in my career.

In the New Testament, Paul is supported by Barnabas in his ministry work. Barnabas, which means 'son of encouragement', is one of my favourite characters in the Bible. He was clearly a significant person and great role model for Paul. In Acts 11:23-24 we read about Barnabas' character when he is sent to Antioch. Having arrived, 'he encouraged them all to remain true to the Lord with all their hearts. He was a good man, full of the Holy Spirit and faith, and a great number of people were brought to the Lord'.

He was one of the first people to come alongside Paul and vouch for him with the other disciples who were unsettled by Paul's conversion (Acts 9:26-28). He stood up for Paul in Acts 11 and acts as a mentor as they work and travel together (Acts 13-15). Barnabas was a great encouragement to Paul. He provided invaluable advice and guidance from the perspective of someone who worked in ministry and mission already. Paul could look up to Barnabas, ask his advice, seek his council as someone who really knows what it's like at the missionary coal face.

David's Role Models

David, spoke about his role models when he was growing up. He says,

> *"My father was really interested in gardening and had a passion for it. Also, there were two men who were neighbours of ours who really enjoyed making their gardens look nice. Being outside and seeing men who were taking care of their gardens made this seem natural and appealing for me. It was a big part of my life."*

Sue's Role Models

In conversation with Sue, she talked about going to the Christian Union at school.

> *"The person who ran it was the Deputy Head and he always stood up for Jesus. He would avoid a lot of the waffle and cut to the chase. He was unfailingly supportive, in terms of helping me build my faith. So he was a really good role model."*

There was a big smile on her face as she said, *"He's quite a character",* clearly still admiring him as a role model. She also sites her Head of Department as a huge role model for her at work, saying,

> *"He's a Christian who is unfailingly kind, unfailingly fair, unfailingly supportive, and will do whatever he can to help. Nobody's perfect, but he really models his faith. He doesn't necessarily talk a lot about his faith to people who aren't Christians, but he does constantly model Christ in everything he does."*

I asked her what she had learnt from him.

> *"Trying to help others flourish is definitely something I've learned from him, having seen his kindness and selflessness in helping others thrive. He looks out for other people and sees how he can help where he can. No matter what water has gone under the bridge before, he is unfailingly kind. Another thing he does, bearing in mind he's probably one of the busiest people I know and works phenomenally hard, is he holds his time quite loosely. He's happy for God to change his agenda, as in his diary, so he's always waiting for God to give him an opportunity to bump into someone in the corridor and change the flow of the day. He's happy to listen to God along the way and then has conversations he wouldn't otherwise have had if he hadn't let God have control of his time. This is something I aspire to, but I don't achieve regularly!"*

Your role models can come from any walk of life. For Sue, her role models are both Christians who seek to demonstrate the love of Jesus in their workplaces. She would turn to both these role models for advice and guidance in her career, and seeks to implement ideas she learned from them. There may be people you don't know personally who can act as a role model for you. You can look to other Christians as trailblazers, aspiring to be more like them. These people are not your idols, they are people you admire and can learn from. Ask yourself:

- Who has worked in the field you are interested in who inspires you?
- What can you learn from their career stories, their successes and failures?
- What skills have they cultivated?
- What do you most admire about them?
- What would you like to emulate?

There are Christians in the world of work who are visible, but if you're not sure where to start, ask your Christian friends. Who do they know? Who do they follow on social media? Consider people who work in similar areas to you, in your sector, in media, in sport, in business, in politics. Research their careers:

- What did they do?
- What decisions did they make?
- What qualities do they have?
- What sets them apart from other people who are not Christians?

Remember God made each of us to be unique, so although you may admire someone and want to follow their example, you will inevitably do 'it' differently and you'll have different results and outcomes. As Christians, we are all the body of Christ, with each of us essential to the full work of building up God's Kingdom (1 Corinthians 12:12-31).

So, go exploring, find out what other Christians are doing in their careers. Follow them on LinkedIn, Facebook, Instagram or Twitter.

I recommend you create a role model collage by choosing the features you admire from different people which impress you. This could be their qualities, their values, their skills or something authentic you notice about them. You can draw inspiration from Christians who are still alive as well as those who have already gone to heaven.

Activity 8: Your Role Models

- Who are your role models?

Make a note of the people who initially come to mind.

- What do you admire most about them?
- How could you emulate this in your own career?

Consider well known Christians you admire for the work they do or the impact they have in their sphere of influence.

Note down the names of one or two and commit to researching their careers.

Follow them on their social media platforms.

List the qualities, skills, or values you most admire.

- How could you grow in one of these areas in your own career and what difference would this make?

Prayer

Father God, thank You for the role models You have planted in my career, help me to learn from them. Father God also bring to mind Christians from the wider world who I can draw inspiration from for my future career.

In Jesus name, Amen.

REFLECTION ACTIVITY: YOUR CIRCLES OF RELATIONSHIPS

God made us relational beings, created for connection with Him and also with other people. Relationships are important for your wellbeing and also for your career. It's often obvious who your trusted friends are, the people you can rely on for support and advice. Next, there is your wider network and the people God is connecting you to for now and for the future. Then there are your role models, those known to you personally, and those not known personally but who you can learn from by their Christian example.

On a large piece of paper draw four concentric circles.

- Put God in the centre circle.
- Write the names of your trusted friends in the next circle. This could be a few or up to a dozen.
- Write the names of people in your wider network in the third circle. These could be people from church, your work, your wider friendship group, people you know outside of work socially. You can copy them from your spidergram or start from scratch. You might find you don't need to record them all, just the ones God brings to mind.
- Make a note of your role models in the fourth circle. You are likely to have between one and three personally known to you.
- Also make a note of any Christians you don't know personally, but you admire for the work they do that you would like to emulate. You could use a different colour for these people.

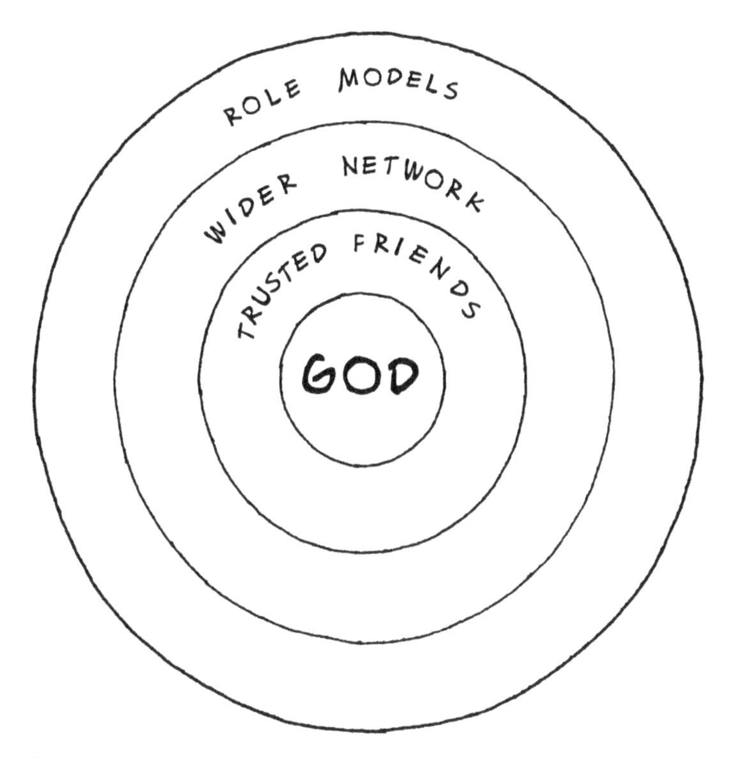

Then consider these questions:

Your Relationship with God.

- What could you do to strengthen your relationship with God?
- Could you spend more time in prayer, reading your Bible, join a fellowship group? Or, could you find time to go for a walk with God, and enjoy His creation with Him?
- What could you commit to? 40 days of Prayer for Your Career or something else?
- How will you confirm what you think God is saying to you?

Your Relationship with your Trusted Friends.

- What is the quality of your relationship with them?
- Do they encourage and champion you?
- How much time could you commit to spending with them?
- Where can you make a note of anything significant they say about your career?

Your Wider Network.

- Who are the people relevant to me?
- What is the quality of my relationship with them?
- What would I like my relationship with them to be like?
- How can I find out more about their work?

Your Role Models.

- What do these people do?
- Why do you admire them?
- What would you like to emulate?
- What could you learn from them?
- How could you use this knowledge in your own career journey?

Prayer

Father God, thank You for fostering relationships, and for Your nurture loving community. Help me to identify the key relationships around You for my career.

In Jesus name, Amen.

GRACE

Gifts
Relationships
Abilities
Curiosities
Experiences

TALENTS
SKILLS
STRENGTHS

Chapter Three: ABILITIES

'For we are God's handiwork, created in Christ Jesus to do good works, which God prepared in advance for us to do'.

(Ephesians 2:10)

You are God's handiwork. He made you with unique **Talents, Skills** and **Strengths** designed specifically to do the work He planned for you. When you find this work, you are walking in God's calling on your life. This is amazing! God loves to reveal Himself to us and, as you explore the abilities He has given you and discover more about yourself you will see God's handiwork in your life.

God's **GRACE** for your career doesn't come in neat boxes. There are blurred edges and overlaps, just as God didn't make people to fit into neat boxes. He made us to be uniquely different from each other so we would have exactly what we need to do the work He has called us to do. There's an overlap between talents, skills and strengths, with some of the natural gifts identified in Chapter One: GIFTS. This is all part of God's 'handiwork', His blueprint for your life. Over time, the natural gifts God has given you grow into talents, skills and strengths which you can use for God's glory. When you're using the abilities God specifically gave you, you will experience fulfilment and satisfaction and you will know you are doing the work God created you for.

In this chapter, we'll start by looking at your talents, and then as you build on these talents, you'll see how they become skills, and then strengths as you use them more and more. Try not to get too caught up in semantics. This is a process of discovery and revelation and will depend on the stage you have reached in your career and how many years of experience you have gained.

You can grow and develop skills which seem so natural to you without realising they are a skill. For example, I learnt to drive many years ago! At the beginning I fumbled and kangarooed my way down the roads. My instructor, Bert, was fond of shouting, *"Yorkie® Bar"* when I strayed too close to the middle of the road (the penalty required was a Yorkie® Bar!), but gradually with time, my skill grew so I didn't have to think about positioning the car on the road anymore. I have developed this skill even more over time, to become a competent driver, as well as my own love of Yorkie® bars!

Talents can become skills, and skills can become strengths. However, strengths might also be evident in the way you use a specific skill or how you behave in situations. This is what makes its use unique to you, as you will discover.

Let's start by looking at the talents God has given to you.

Prayer

Father God, thank You for the many abilities
You have given me, all the talents, skills and
strengths. As I explore them, I ask Your Holy
Spirit to reveal each one to me.

In Jesus name, Amen.

YOUR TALENTS

'For it will be like a man going on a journey, who called his servants and entrusted to them his property. To one he gave five talents, to another two, to another one, to each according to his ability. Then he went away'.

(Matthew 25:14-15 ESV)

Although this parable is often interpreted to mean about investing money it's also about using the talents God has given you to grow His property – His Kingdom. We're each given talents and then expected to use them according to our ability.

Your talents are specific and unique to you. You were born with them. They are the activities which come easily to you, things you do naturally and the ways in which you naturally respond to situations. This is the overlap with your natural gifts. Your talents are God given, building blocks to be developed and strengthened.

Sometimes your talents are displayed as abilities or skills, and sometimes it's your attitudes, your outlooks, the way you are kind to people or animals, your love of the outdoors, your passion for books or painting or for building things.

It could be God has given you musical ability, and you were drawn to music as a child. You might have made a noise, you might have hummed all the time, you might have been intrigued by how sounds are made. You loved the patterns in music you heard and as you grew up you had lessons and learnt how to read music and how to make sounds which corresponded to the musical patterns on the paper. Your musical ability was nurtured through learning an instrument.

Initially, your sounds might have been laboured and jagged but the more you practiced the more fluent you became until your talent for musicality transformed into a skill in playing a specific instrument. Now, the more you play and the more you practice the more proficient you become; and this skill becomes a strength!

We can't all enter talent competitions so how do you know what your talents are? God gives us clues. Max Lucado calls these *'your sweet spot'*[1] – times in your near and distant past when you did something well and enjoyed doing it, and experienced success and satisfaction.

In Chapter One: GIFTS you reviewed the natural gifts God gave you. When you look back at them which of these do you identify as a particular talent? Can you think of a story of when you used this talent as a child, as a young adult, in different stages of your life? Think about what you enjoyed about these experiences and what you found most satisfying. Try to add as much detail as possible to each story so the memory comes alive for you. Here's one of mine...

When I was a little girl I could get totally absorbed in projects. Aged 9, I was tasked with finding out about Emperor Penguins for a school project. With my family, I visited the Natural History Museum in London, where I saw stuffed Emperor Penguins and picked up an information sheet to use alongside the natural history books we had at home. I was fascinated by the idea that the male penguin is the one who incubates the eggs, and the chicks are born grey and develop their lovely Emperor plumage as they grow (40+ years ago and I still remember this). I spent hours tracing pictures of penguins and colouring them (there was no clipart or copy and paste in those days). I remember carefully writing captions and information alongside the pictures in my neatest handwriting. I was really satisfied with the finished product which looked cheerful and colourful.

Little known to me, our projects were entered into a national competition and I won some natural history resources for our school and also a book, *The World of Wildlife,*[2] published in collaboration with the World Wildlife Fund. I remember standing with the Headmistress during assembly when they announced I had won feeling slightly bemused because creating the pamphlet had seemed effortless and I had enjoyed making it.

When I review this story, the following features become apparent.

- The theme of animals again! Note the Emperor Penguins. Remember my love of animals when I was reviewing my natural gifts?
- Being absorbed by writing and creating a booklet and spending time making it look nice.
- I even remember planning it out, so I knew what was going to be on each page.

This talent was honed as a teenager over several school projects, but the one which really comes alive for me is creating the Emperor Penguin pamphlet because I was so absorbed in it.

As an adult, whenever I have a project to create, a report to write or a talk or presentation to prepare I rely on these talents God has given me and I know this because I find myself absorbed in the process. This story also provides early evidence of my skills and strengths as I'll explain later.

Matt's Talents

Matt, a self-employed painter and decorator loved being outdoors as a child,

"I guess I was always active. I was constantly out on my bike with my friends or roller skating on the seafront; I loved climbing trees. I played a lot of music as a kid. Music was a big part of life through school.

After school, I had a year out and went to work in a boarding school which had about four or five people like me, called Gap students. The role was varied and included a day a week working out on the grounds, cutting grass and general maintenance. We would provide cover for absent staff doing a bit of teaching and because it was a boarding school, we ran lots of activities for the kids in the evenings and at weekends; great fun, and I loved it. Then, I went and did Camp America[3] through the summer, which was fantastic and again I loved it.

At university I did Geography, allegedly! Basically, I played hockey. So, I ended up getting a 3rd and probably would have been a 1st if I had a hockey degree! I just had fun and a great time. I realised the academic study wasn't ever my particular forte. It was about the sports and the people, team games and being outdoors.

Then my life went properly outdoors! I visited a friend who was doing a ski season and I just fell in love with the whole idea of working in a ski resort, so when I left Uni' this is what I did! One season ended up being five, including summer seasons in a beach resort where I ended up teaching water sports."

Matt's talents are clear! Being active outdoors, playing team games and sport.

Talents are the foundation for your skills and strengths and as you read on you will discover how your talents have been honed as skills and grown into strengths. This is all a part of the **GRACE** God has given you for your career.

So, what are some of your talent stories?

Activity 9: Your Talent Stories

To help you look for clues for your talents, review the natural gifts you identified in Chapter One: GIFTS. Add specific details of particular events when you felt totally absorbed in something and had a positive result which you found satisfying.

Pray for God to prompt you with reminders of stories which illustrate your talents.

Recall a few times when you were totally absorbed in something as a child. You could review your list of natural gifts and think of specific examples or occasions where you were totally absorbed. This should be a specific event, not a generalised activity.

Next, tell the story of what happened in each specific occasion or example. Describe what happened in as much detail as you can remember. The more detail you can remember the better. You can use the following questions as a prompt, but don't just answer the questions – tell your story in your own words!

- What happened?
- What were you doing?

- Who was there?
- What was the occasion?
- What did you specifically enjoy?
- How did you feel?
- How do you know you were absorbed?
- What was the result or outcome which you found so satisfying?

Now, it's time to look for clues! Go back over what you have written with a highlighter and mark any words which really resonate with you, whether they are verbs, nouns, environments, or feelings.

Make a note of any patterns or repetitions.

When you spot a talent use a few words or a sentence or two to describe what this talent is.

Note: - rather than writing, find an app to record your stories orally and then transcribe automatically.

Sometimes our talents lie dormant and are not fully realised until we are adults. Try this exercise again for a time when you were totally absorbed in something as an adult. These can be examples from any area of your life or work. Remember, each example should be a specific event, not a generalised activity. Use as much detail as you can remember to flesh out your story using the questions above as a guide.

Prayer

Father God, thank You for the talents You have given me, please reveal them to me as I consider what they are.

In Jesus name, Amen.

YOUR SKILLS

'Also I have given ability to all the skilled workers to make everything I have commanded you'.

(Exodus 31:6b)

Skills are abilities you use to accomplish a task. They are very much about getting things done, which have an end result, often without realising you are using skills. Skills can be learned and improved through repetition. Many are also transferable, which is really exciting from a career perspective. The challenge is knowing what your skills are, describing them to others and knowing the ones you want to use or develop in the future.

In his book, *How to Get a Job You Love*, John Lees, expert career coach, writes, "Skills are the building blocks of work, the raw material that transforms a job description into activity that creates results".[4]

Let's look at how God gifted people in the Bible with specific skills to use for His glory.

In Exodus, Chapters 25-40, God gives full and detailed instructions about how the Tabernacle (God's sanctuary where He will dwell) is to be built. He includes details for the Ark of the Covenant and its Atonement cover, the table of acacia wood, the lampstand of pure gold, the tabernacle tent with all the upright wooden frames, crossbars, curtains of finely twisted linen, coverings of goat hair, gold hooks, silver bases, altars with accompanying utensils, the huge courtyard. Then there is pressed olive oil needed for the lamps, intricate woven priestly garments, anointing oil, and specific incense to be made. The task is vast in scope and elaborate in its design.

God allocates people He has gifted with specific skills to build the Tabernacle. He appoints Bezalel, a sculptor and fills him with the Spirit of God and with skill, ability and knowledge, 'to make artistic designs for work in gold, silver and bronze, to cut and set stones, to work in wood and to engage in all kinds of crafts' (Exodus 31:4-5). God also appoints Oholiab, 'an engraver and designer, and an embroiderer in blue, purple and scarlet yarn and fine linen' (Exodus 38:23) to help Bezalel. In addition, God gives ability 'to all the skilled workers to make everything I have commanded you' (Exodus 31:6b).

This wasn't just any old tent they were building. It required a high level of skill including in making the beautiful, twisted linen and intricately embroidered curtains, 'All those who were skilled among the workers made the tabernacle with ten curtains of finely twisted linen and blue, purple and scarlet yarn, with cherubim woven into them by expert hands' (Exodus 36:8).

Bezalel was entrusted with creating the Ark and we read in Exodus 37 the Atonement cover was made of pure gold, with cherubim sculpted into each end, their wings spread upward overshadowing the cover. The lampstand was made of pure gold and had branches, flowerlike cups, buds and blossoms all hammered out of pure gold, with seven lamps, wick trimmers and trays of pure gold. It must have been exquisitely beautiful.

We are told about some of the skills required in Exodus 39, crafting, weaving, embroidering. These verses describe not only what needed to be done, but also how well it was to be done! The implication is, not only did the weavers need to know how to weave, but they also needed to weave to a high standard.

By my rough reckoning, people with many different skills were needed to build the Tabernacle: designer, engraver, embroiderer, carpenters, weavers, sowers, tailors, smelters, blacksmiths. It would also have required people to harvest and press olives, perfumers to make the incense, people to weave the linen and make the goat's hair coverings, goat herders to look after the goats, carpenters to make the frames, metal workers to make the utensils and lampstand.

God gave these skills to His people to build His sanctuary. In addition, all these skilled people needed to work together so project management, teamwork, communication, organising, scheduling, managing resources, delegating and supervising would have been required as well. You can see how quickly the list of skills can be built up.

Let's consider the skills of an individual so you can start to identify your own.

King David was a man of many skills, grown from his natural gifts which I described in Chapter One: GIFTS. At first, he was a shepherd, skilled at looking after sheep, finding them pasture and water, shearing them, probably birthing lambs as well protecting them from danger and wild animals. He would be using organising skills, planning skills, caring and nurturing skills, self-awareness skills, practical skills and physical skills.

We know he was also a skillful musician, since many of the Psalms are attributed to him and he is taken into King Saul's service to soothe him by playing the lyre. 'One of the servants answered, "I have seen a son of Jesse of Bethlehem who knows how to play the lyre. He is a brave man and a warrior" (1 Samuel 16:18a). This is borne out as David faces

Goliath, the giant Philistine who mocks the Israelites, slaying him with courage and single-mindedness. (1 Samuel 17:45- 50)

With great insight, David explains how his transferable skills will help him win against Goliath. 'David said to Saul, "Your servant has been keeping his father's sheep. When a lion or a bear came and carried off a sheep from the flock, I went after it, struck it and rescued the sheep from its mouth. When it turned on me, I seized it by its hair, struck it and killed it. Your servant has killed both the lion and the bear; this uncircumcised Philistine will be like one of them, because he has defied the armies of the living God"' (1 Samuel 17:34-36). God was honing David's talents as a shepherd into important skills to use in the future.

Sometime later, David has to flee for his life, and his leadership skills begin to emerge, as 'All those who were in distress or in debt or discontented gathered around him, and he became their commander. Around four hundred men were with him' (1 Samuel 22:2). As the story unfolds, David's leadership skills grow, taking responsibility for people who suffer because of King Saul's actions, seeking God's counsel for his own actions and strategies, learning how to negotiate with both allies and enemies, forming alliances, caring for people's material needs and wellbeing, and speaking with wisdom.

After Saul's death, David becomes King of Judah, and then King of Israel where he fortifies the City of Jerusalem and recovers the Ark of the Covenant. The leadership skills he developed when he led a flock of sheep have had to expand and grow into something much bigger as King of Israel. This happened gradually as he went from leading the four hundred men, to leading armies fighting the Philistines, to leading the procession as the Ark returned to Jerusalem (2 Samuel 6) and then leading the Kingdom of Israel.

The skills he needed as King would include communicating, influencing, challenging others, motivating others, strategising, developing worship, delegating to all of his officials, 'mighty men, warriors, priests, singers, gatekeepers, treasurers, overseers, counsellors' as detailed in 1 Chronicles 11-27, as well as administering 'justice and righteousness' (2 Samuel 8:15 NASB). In this time, he also grew his musicianship skills, writing more Psalms of worship and thanks. The songs he might have sung on the mountainside when he was a shepherd made way for songs like David's Song of Thanks in 1 Chronicles 16:7-36 ESV.

All of David's skills were from God, and God uses David to build up His people Israel. David was given success in using his skills for a purpose. 'In everything he did he had great success, because the Lord was with him' (1 Samuel 18:14).

There is so much you can do when you know what your skills are. You can improve them and grow them, you can learn new ones, you can stop using those you're not particularly good at. It's really well worth taking time to explore your skills, asking God what He thinks, and then talking to one of your trusted friends about what they think your skills are. Which ones are your core skills, lesser skills, enjoyable skills, transferable skills?

In the world of work, there are many skills and many skill mixes and levels of proficiency. These skills fall into different categories such as creative, practical, technical, people related, processing, leadership, and personal.

Here's how I identified my skills:

My current role: Career Coach

I wrote down some of the skills I use... listening, questioning, empathising, challenging, giving feedback, intuition, rapport building, persistence.

Then I delved a bit deeper with some of these skills.

What is it about my listening skills that make me an effective career coach? Is it because I listen with full attention, noticing non-verbal cues as well as spoken words?

When I ask coaching questions, I might frame them in a way which gets clients to think without feeling judged.

These are skills which I transferred from my previous role as a learning and development consultant, but which I now use in a more focused way. I also combine them, for example, I might ask a client a 'check question' on an assumption and then watch them whilst listening to their reply. Often, I can draw from what they're not saying as much as I can from the words they do speak.

In the future, I might want to grow my questioning skills by learning how to ask really powerful questions which will enhance the coaching experience for the client.

I also run my own business and the skills I need for this include planning and organising, strategising, marketing, networking etc. I've had a very steep learning curve in-terms of social media marketing including what content to write and share, what platforms to use, how to grow followers ... a whole new skillset I've had to learn.

Writing this book has involved researching, writing, editing, interviewing, reviewing, planning and organising.

Some skills are specifically related to a particular career sphere and others are transferable. It can be quite a challenge to identify your skills, so I recommend a multi-layered approach. Remember, you use skills in all aspects of your life and sometimes it's helpful to explore the skills you use outside of your current career, in voluntary roles, leisure activities or even in your homelife.

Jenny's Skills

A recent client of mine, Jenny, was involved in many voluntary activities outside of work and as she explored the skills she used in these roles, it filled her with excitement and helped build her confidence to see her skills as a fantastic resource for her future career. She found she was not limited by the current skills she is using at work, but she had potential to use other skills which were lying dormant. She comments,

> *"Volunteering as a charity trustee (of my village primary school parent-teacher association and then the local Scout group) gave me understanding of fiduciary responsibilities. I learned how to confidently chair meetings, deal with conflict and organise and run large events using volunteers. Being a trustee built upon existing skills I had gained through work as a project manager and also provided satisfaction in knowing I was making a significant contribution to improving my community."*

God also fills His people with His Spirit for the workplace so that when they use their skills, other people are impacted beyond our expectations. Remember Bezalel; he was filled with the Spirit of God as well as being a skilled craftsman. God says, "I've filled him with the Spirit of God, giving him skill and know-how and expertise in every kind of craft to create designs ... he's an all-round craftsman" (Exodus 31:3 MSG).

Nicky Gumbel writes, "It is possible to be a talented musician, writer or artist without being filled with the Spirit. But when the Spirit of God fills people for these tasks their work often takes on a new dimension. It has far greater spiritual impact. This can be true even where the natural ability of the musician or artist is not particularly outstanding. Hearts can be touched, and lives changed."[5] No doubt something like this happened through Bezalel. The Holy Spirit took his skills to another level.

This can also be seen in the life of Moses. When he encounters God in the burning bush and is commissioned to bring the Israelites out of Egypt, he protests, "Master, please, I don't talk well. I've never been good with words, neither before nor after you spoke to me. I stutter and stammer" (Exodus 4:10 MSG). Moses insists he isn't eloquent and he struggles to find the right words and stumbles his way through talking.

And yet, God uses him, firstly to speak to Pharoah, via Aaron, and then on his own as he leads the Israelites for 40 years in the desert. He preaches the longest sermon in the Old Testament; most of Deuteronomy is Moses speaking to the people, instructing them in the ways they should live their lives. By the time he dies, he recites a beautiful song inspired by and in praise of God (Deuteronomy 31:30).

So even when you think you might not be particularly skilled at something God can use you and grow and develop this skill for His glory. How might the Holy Spirit be using the skills he's given you above and beyond your expectations? As you compile your list of skills, let God speak to you about the ones

He wants you to use. Pray about your skills and notice which ones make your heart quicken, which ones seem appealing to you. Sit with this for a few days and then go back to review your skills bank. Do you feel the same prompting?

Activity 10: Create Your Skills Bank

Start with some prayer! Identifying your skills can be a big task so ask God to go before you to reveal the skills He wants.

Take a large piece of paper, A3 or Flip Chart, and a stack of post-it notes. Or use an online whiteboard or workspace.

Then consider your current role.

- What are the skills you use each day?

Jot them down on the post-it notes as they come to mind.

Then make a note of any activities, jobs or volunteering you may do or have done outside paid employment.

- What skills were you using?

Consider the skills you've used in the past, both work and non-work related. Write these down as well.

Organise these skills into groups under headings such as Creative or People or Personal or Technical skills. Consider ones which go naturally together.

Then, rank them in order of proficiency.

- How good are you at this skill?
- Are there some skills you don't want to use anymore? Cast them aside

Now, highlight the ones you want to use more in the future.

- How could you grow and develop these skills?

Talk this through with a close friend, colleague or career coach, so you don't get overwhelmed.

You should end up with a big 'bank' of skills which you can draw upon.

Some will excite you; some might surprise you; all will be useful for your work and career.

Prayer

Father God, thank You for the many skills
You have blessed me with. Please prompt my
thoughts as I consider my skills and how I
might use them and grow them for Your glory.

In Jesus name, Amen.

YOUR STRENGTHS

'The joy of the Lord is your strength'.
(Nehemiah 8:10b)

A strength begins with a talent. As you grow your talents with time, learning, knowledge and practice they become strengths. Sometimes your strengths grow from specific skills; and at other times your strengths come from specific characteristics unique to you; the way you 'do' things, the innate part of who you are and how you behave, such as kindness or courage or sensitivity.

For example, as a child you might have had a natural enthusiasm for showing objects to people. Remember your natural gifts! You didn't have to learn this, it just came naturally. In time you went to school and channelled your natural inclination for showing things to people, or sharing ideas, into teaching skills and became qualified as a Teacher! Your Strength is in explaining things clearly to people. When you are explaining things, you find time flies by. You could keep on explaining and finding more ways to put your point across. You love seeing people respond to your explaining and this gives you energy and satisfaction. This is an innate tendency you had as a child which has developed into a strength as you have used it more and more.

In the Parable of the Talents, as the Master heads off on a journey he gives his servants talents according to their ability. When he returns, he rewards the servants who have grown their talents and gives them more (Matthew 25:20-23). The implication is clear, God wants you to use your talents, to invest in them, so they grow into strengths. Imagine your strengths as equivalent to five talents!

When we think of strength we often think of physical strength. This was true of Samson in the Bible (Judges 13-16). However, your strengths are so much more than this. When you use your strengths, they build you up and help you perform at your best. This could be strengths in the way you use your skills, or strengths in your character and how this is revealed in your work and career.

Let me give you some more examples from the Bible.

The prophet Samuel had spiritual strength, relying on God to direct his steps. 'Samuel grew up. God was with him, and Samuel's prophetic record was flawless. Everyone in Israel, from Dan in the north to Beersheba in the south, recognized Samuel was the real thing—a true prophet of God' (1 Samuel 3:19-20 MSG).

Ruth, the Moabitess, displays strength of loyalty when she refuses to abandon her mother-in-law, Naomi. 'But Ruth replied, "Don't urge me to leave you or to turn back from you. Where you go I will go, and where you stay I will stay. Your people will be my people and your God my God"' (Ruth 1:16). Throughout the book of Ruth, she demonstrates her loyalty strength as she travels with Naomi, gleans in the fields and talks respectfully to Boaz, whilst taking care of her mother-in-law.

John the Baptist displays strength in his sense of purpose, his mission to get the Israelites to repent and be baptised, to prepare the way for the Lord. This sense of purpose was displayed in what he wore and ate, as well as the words he preached. 'John's clothes were made of camel's hair, and he had a leather belt round his waist. His food was locusts and wild honey. People went out to him from Jerusalem and all Judea and the whole region of the Jordan. Confessing their sins, they were baptised by him in the River Jordan' (Matthew 3:4-6).

I'm a big fan of knowing and using your strengths. There are lots of online tools to help you discover yours and the one I particularly like is Strengths Profile©.[6] This is an online assessment which provides you with a personal profile based on your performance, energy and use of your strengths, across four quadrants including:

- Realised Strengths – strengths you use and enjoy.
- Learned Behaviours – things you've learned to do well but may not enjoy.
- Weaknesses – things you find hard and don't enjoy.
- Unrealised Strengths – strengths you don't use as often but would really benefit from using more – these are your hidden talents!

The profile gives you a clear understanding of your realised strengths, your key strengths, which really energise you when you use them and help you to thrive. It identifies your learned behaviours, which drain you of energy and it pinpoints your weaknesses, things you should avoid doing. The profile also exposes your unrealised strengths, your hidden talents, so you can consider how you might use these more to gain energy and fulfilment in your career.

Some of your strengths are innate and others are skills or talents you have grown and developed into strengths over time. How you use your strengths might vary from time to time. Your answers to the online questionnaire are likely to be reliant on your current situation. There are 60 strengths defined in the Strengths Profile© and you can find them listed, along with their definitions, in Appendix Two. The report from the online assessment will highlight those most key at this moment in time.

Knowing and understanding your realised strengths, is invaluable. When you use them, you will flourish and achieve without having to rely on your learned behaviours, which may drain you of energy. You can explore how to embrace your unrealised strengths to grow and develop fully utilising the talents God gave you.

In a recent Strengths Profile debrief session with my client, Jenny, she noticed a *'lightbulb moment'* when she understood she wasn't using one of her unrealised strengths, '**Adventure**'. She recognised how energised she would feel if she was able to use this in her career. Her enthusiasm levels rose as she considered how she might use this strength in the future.

The picture opposite shows a copy of my Introductory Profile in 2020. My top realised strength is **'Mission'**. When I am using my 'Mission' strength and pursuing things which give me a sense of meaning and purpose then I am fully energized, focused and fired up!

However, when I'm using my top learned behaviour of **'Adherence'** I find I become drained more easily and the work doesn't flow, because even though I am good at following processes this doesn't energise me. I am more creative, energised and relaxed when I'm in 'Mission' mode and therefore achieve so much more!

Remember as a child I was always running to get to where I wanted to go to get results? Looking back, I can see the 'golden thread' between this natural gift, the skills I have developed to help me get from A to B without physically

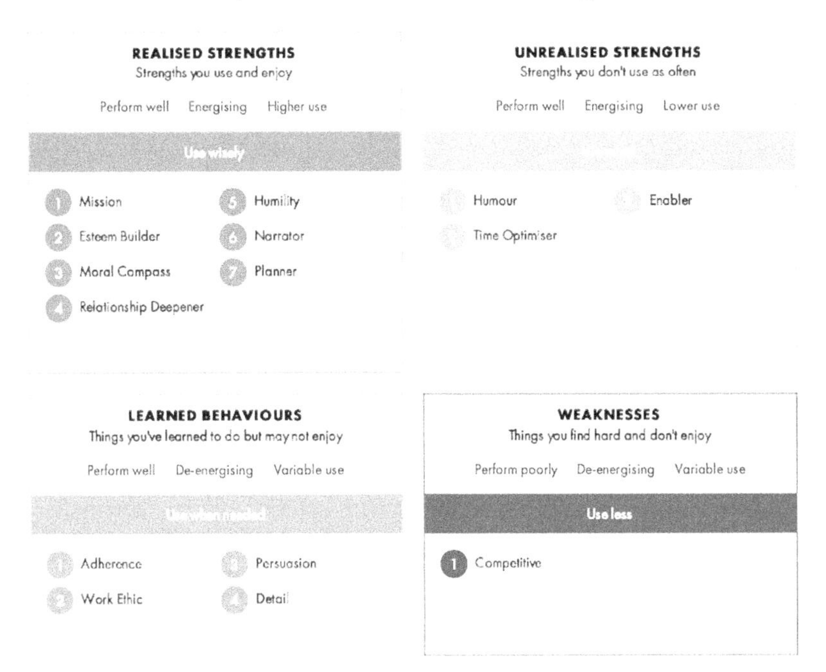

My Introductory Profile (dated 5-12-20)

running, and the fully fledged 'Mission' strength realised in me now. I can see God's hand in the way he knit me together in my mother's womb and how this has developed from childhood until now. In fact, if you had asked people who knew me well when I was growing up, I'm sure they'd have said, *"Katie's always on a mission!"*

And then there's **'Relationship Deepener'**. Remember my love of animals as a child? This has grown from my love of developing relationships with animals to being able to invest the time and energy into developing deep relationships with people. I don't have to make a conscious effort to make this happen, because I feel energised when I spend time with people with whom I've developed lasting relationships.

As for my unrealised strengths, my hidden talents waiting to be grown, I love the idea I can be an **'Enabler'** and I can feel the energy rising in me as I consider how I might use this strength to help other people with their careers. Just imagine what I could achieve by combining my 'Enabler' strength with my 'Mission' strength!

You'll also see **'Competitive'** is a weakness for me. I am not motivated by competition; in fact, it drains me. I'd much rather collaborate with people, using my 'Relationship Deepener' strength, to co-operate with them rather than compete with them. Even my family tell me I'm not a good competitor, because I gloat too much when I win at Monopoly, and everyone leaves the room feeling miserable!

Here are some more examples from the Bible, using some Strengths Profile descriptors.

The prophet Nathan used his **'Moral Compass'** strength when he rebuked David about his affair with Bathsheba. Nathan was driven to do what was right in God's eyes and to point out David's misdemeanours. He probably also used his **'Explainer'** strength, the ability to *'simplify things so others can understand'*. He does this to great effect in his storytelling about the man who has a large number of sheep yet steals the poor man's only and most loved ewe lamb. David is left in no doubt Nathan is referring to his own sinful actions. No further explanation is needed (2 Samuel 12:1-14).

In the book of Esther, we read of Queen Esther who had immense strength of '**Courage**' to approach King Xerxes in support of her people at great personal risk to her own life. The 'Courage' strength definition is being able to *'overcome your fears and do what you want to do in spite of them.'* Anyone who approached the King uninvited could be put to death unless he extended his gold sceptre to them. Esther knew this and yet she courageously chose to approach him because of the plight of her people (Esther 4:11). She continues to display immense 'Courage' as she invites the King and Haman, the man who is trying to destroy the Israelites, to sumptuous banquets, so she can present her request to save the Jews to the King (Esther 1-7).

Some of your strengths are innate and others are skills or talents you have grown and developed into strengths over time which means you can adapt to the situation you are in and use strengths that are pertinent to your context and you will find your strengths rise and fall depending on your current role and circumstances.

Every time I complete my profile online, I expect to see 'Mission', 'Relationship Deepener' and 'Narrator' in my top seven, because these are innate to me. Circumstances and what I am focusing on in my career determines which others rise to the fore. As you might expect my **'Writer'** strength has risen to the top of my realised strengths in the last profile I completed (Feb 2022). This wasn't in the top seven for the profile I did in December 2020 because I hadn't started writing this book.

Sue's Strengths

I conducted a Strengths Profile debrief with Sue. She has been a doctor for many years and there were times when she felt she was really thriving and times when she wasn't. She says,

> *"When I first became a consultant, I had this incredible opportunity to develop a service from scratch, which was amazing. It was really hard work and quite daunting,*

> *but I flourished doing it, developing a service which is really good for patients and is patient-centred care".*

Looking back, she noticed she was thriving because she was combining her realised strengths including **'Creativity', 'Resolver', 'Catalyst',** and **'Innovation'** to generate all the ideas for the service. She also commented on the *"fantastic team of incredible colleagues around me helping to develop the service."* You might guess, **'Humility'** is another realised strength and Sue finds it really energising to credit other people for the success of the service as well.

Sue also spoke about a time when she found she was using her learned behaviours more than her realised strengths and the impact this had on her,

> *"More recently, I've had a period of time where I've had to cover for a colleague, who has been off work for a while, and so the creative aspect of my role has been put on hold. I've literally been at the coalface, delivering care rather than developing service. What happened was I started to rely on my learned behaviours, which are* **Detail, Adherence, Work Ethic.** *These are all things I do well, but I don't derive any energy from using them. This meant for the past nine months I was very depleted and running low in energy. Now my colleague has returned and I have the opportunity to do some more innovation and service development. This means I feel invigorated by my work again."*

So, what are your strengths?

When you are clear about what your strengths are you can begin to play to them, at work and in your career, to help you flourish every day. Knowing your strengths can also help in your job search, distinguishing you from other candidates and building your energy and confidence, so you perform well at interviews. When you're faced with the dreaded question, *"Tell me about your strengths?"* or *"What are your weaknesses?"* you'll be armed with stories to tell.

A client of mine, Lee, was asked in a second interview for a job, *"We know you can do the job, but why should we appoint you rather than someone else?"* He was able to talk with ease and energy about his unrealised strengths, because he knew what they were, and he felt energised when he considered using them in a work setting. As a result he was offered the job!

It's really worth the time and effort to unpack your strengths, to be fully cognisant of the five talents God has given you so you can use them to full effect. But a word of caution – as with all the other questionnaires and profiles – remember you are unique! You can use different combinations of your strengths, combined with your skills and your personality to conduct the work God prepared for you in any way.

Don't lose heart if you are not playing to your strengths, keep pressing on. Our strength is in the Lord! When we are weak, He is strong. He strengthens us. As Paul writes, 'But He said to me, "My grace is sufficient for you, for my power is made perfect in weakness." Therefore, I will boast all the more gladly about my weaknesses, so that Christ's power may rest on me' (2 Corinthians 12:9).

This is one of the wonderful paradoxes of the Christian faith. God has created us each with a unique combination of talents, skills and strengths and yet, He works through our weaknesses and inabilities.

Stepping out in faith is more important to Him, than waiting until we are fully equipped. He supplies the things we are deficient in, whether it's working with other people with complementary skills, miraculous provision, providential timing or serendipitous meetings, all arranged through the Holy Spirit, so we use our talents, skills, and strengths for His glory.

Activity 11: Complete your Strengths Profile© online

You can do your own Free Starter Profile at www.strengthsprofile.com.

- What did you find out about yourself?
- What, if anything, really resonated with you?

Your Realised Strengths

- What delights you about your realised strengths?
- Which are you most proud of?
- Which would you like to be known for?
- Which are serving you best in your current role?
- How might you use a combination of your realised strengths in a way that is unique to you?

Your Learned Behaviours

- How do you feel about your learned behaviours?
- Is there one you are using too much which you

need to put down?

- How reliant are you on your learned behaviours in your current role?
- What action could you take to become less reliant?
- Are you relying on any learned behaviours which are draining your energy?

Your Weaknesses

- How are you going to stop using your weaknesses, the things which drain you?
- Are there strengths in the other three quadrants you could use instead?

Your Unrealised Strengths

- Which unrealised strength would you like to dial up?
- What one way could you increase usage of your unrealised strengths to boost your energy in your career?
- Which of your unrealised strengths could you develop by using more? How might you do this?

Your Super Strength

- How could you combine your realised strengths with your unrealised strengths to promote their use?

Prayer

Father God, thank You for the talents You gave me which have grown into strengths to energise me and help me flourish. Help me to develop the unrealised strengths, the hidden talents You have gifted me with.

In Jesus name, Amen.

REFLECTION ACTIVITY: YOUR GOLDEN THREADS

God gifted you uniquely with talents, skills and strengths and He wants you to use them. During your exploration, you will have found there are themes and ideas which are repeated, threads connecting your talents, skills and strengths. I like to call them, '*golden threads.*' This is where you can see the talents God "knitted together" in you, which have developed and grown into skills and then strengths. You will also have an idea of the skills and strengths you want to build on for the future.

Take a moment to reflect on the abilities God has given you.

Review your Talent Stories

- What are your key talents? Jot down single words or a sentence or two to act as a reminder.

Consider Your Skills Bank

- What are your top 5 skills – these are skills you are most proficient in?
- Which skills do you not want to use any more?
- Which skills do you want to use more?
- What skills do you want to develop or learn?
- How do you feel God prompting you to use your skills through the power of His Holy Spirit?

Reflect on Your Strengths

- What are your key strengths? How could you use them more?

- Which learned behaviours are you going to rely on less so you feel less drained?
- What will you do instead of using your weaknesses?
- How will you use your unrealised strengths, your hidden talents more?
- What do you think God might be saying to you about your talents, skills and strengths?

Prayer

Father God, thank You for all the abilities You have given me. Help me to use the talents, skills and strengths You have given me and help me to develop and grow the ones I need for my future career.

In Jesus name, Amen.

GRACE

Gifts
Relationships
Abilities
Curiosities
Experiences

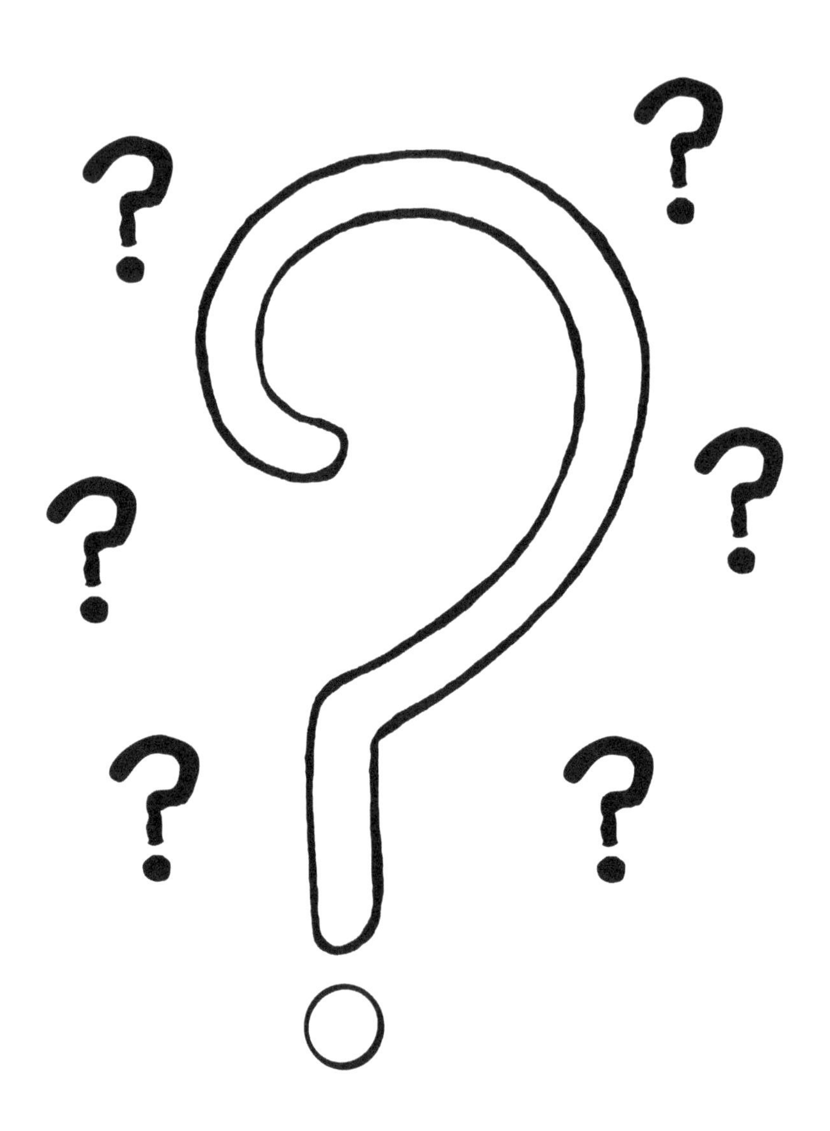

Chapter Four: CURIOSITIES

'Through Him all things were made; without Him nothing was made that has been made'.

(John 1:3)

God's creation is awesome and there is so much for us to learn. He has hidden clues for us to find and He reveals things to us all the time. The topics you are curious about give you clues about what He might be hiding for you to find. You might discover it in:

- Your **Education** - the subjects you chose to study.
- Your **Knowledge** - gained through living life.
- Your **Interests** - the topics in which you are keenly interested.
- Your **Compassion** - the causes you care deeply about.
- Your **Inner Wisdom** - the ideas you feel God has put on your heart.
- Your **Revelations from God** - the insights He has revealed to you through His word, prophecies or other people.

This chapter is about exploring how your curiosities could lead to career ideas.

In his book, *How to Get a Job you Love,* John Lees, a career expert, notes the importance of 'curiosity' in your career search. He suggests when curiosity is combined with 'optimism', you are compelled to explore options, push on open doors and pursue ideas which interest you.[1] The things you are curious about can give you an insight into the career options which are right for you, which light a spark of "that sounds interesting," or "I wonder what it would be like ...?"

However, a word of caution. Curiosity needs to be grounded in faith, in God's word and the Holy Spirit, because without this we can be led off the path of righteousness, as Adam and Eve were in the Garden of Eden (Genesis 3). So, I suggest you explore this chapter with a curiosity inspired by God.

King Solomon knew the importance of discernment. This is what he asked for at the beginning of his reign, and God granted him wisdom and insight. 'God gave Solomon wisdom and very great insight, and a breadth of understanding as measureless as the sand on the seashore' (1 Kings 4:29).

Jesus also grew in wisdom, as we read in Luke 2 when, aged 12, He became so absorbed in listening to teachers and questioning them in the Temple in Jerusalem, He missed His family's departure. We are told, 'And Jesus grew in wisdom and stature, and in favour with God and man' (Luke 2:52).

God has made us curious creatures and I'm sure you'll find you are curious about many things, but how do you know which ones lead to what God has planned for you, and which ones don't? I propose you draw a Vine of Curiosity rooted in Jesus.

In John 15 Jesus is described as the vine and believers as the branches. Jesus says, "I am the vine; you are the branches. If you remain in me and I in you, you will bear much fruit; apart from me you can do nothing" (John 15:5). Remain in Jesus, abide in His love, and you will bear much fruit.

I am borrowing this image to help you explore your curiosity so that it is rooted in Jesus, with each branch representing a different area of 'curiosity' in your life and career. Your Vine of Curiosity will be personal to you and it may take time to develop as you consider each of the different sections or branches. You may find some are particularly clear to you whilst others take more discernment and prayer. God is not in a rush, so take your time as you let your curiosity grow in your vine.

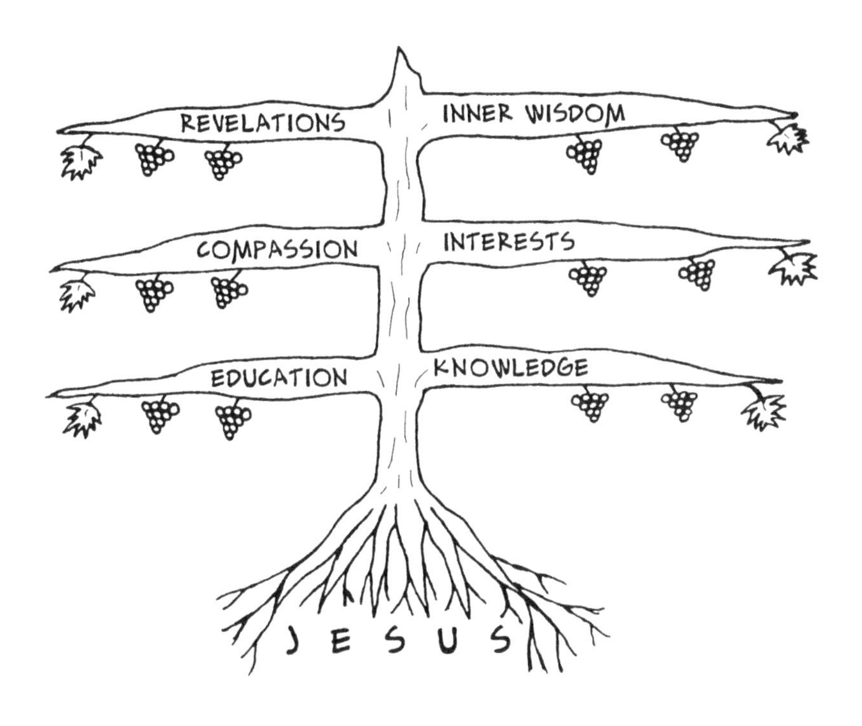

Vine of Curiosity

At the end of the chapter there are instructions provided so you can create your own Vine of Curiosity, but in the meantime, the following sections will help you gather information for each branch. There will be a branch for your Education, your Knowledge, your Interests, your Compassion (things you care about), your Inner Wisdom (things buried deep in your heart) and your Revelations from God. There are suggested activities to help you flesh out your thoughts in each area before you decide what will go on your Vine.

As you read further on in the passage in John 15, you'll read that God prunes His vine. When you have gathered all your information there will be an opportunity for pruning before you populate your own Vine of Curiosity. But for now, don't worry about pruning, let your mind explore your curiosities freely allowing yourself to gather as much information as you like.

I recommend using a notebook or setting up a specific online file to record the ideas for your branches from each section before putting the pertinent things on your own Vine of Curiosity at the end of the chapter. You may find you need to set aside a considerable amount of time to consider each area and then come back to them in the pruning process. Remember, there's no rush, so take your time.

Prayer

Father God, thank You for the curiosity You have given me. Please prompt me as I consider the things I am curious about. Help me to discard the things which are not from You and take note of the things which are from You.

In Jesus name, Amen.

YOUR EDUCATION

'Above all and before all, do this: Get Wisdom!
Write this at the top of your list: Get Understanding!'
(Proverbs 4:7 MSG)

God uses people who are fully educated as well as those who are not. He is not limited by what you did or didn't learn at school. In His eyes, your education is much broader. Often, He will use people before they are fully trained or educated.

In the Bible, Peter, a simple fisherman, becomes a man of God and the leader of the early Church. God uses him mightily. Filled with the Holy Spirit, he preaches an amazing sermon on the day of Pentecost (Acts 2:14-40), despite his lack of formal education.

Paul, a well-educated man, also becomes a humble man of God. He says, "I am a Jew, born in Tarsus of Cilicia, but brought up in this city. I studied under Gamaliel and was thoroughly trained in the law of our ancestors. I was just as zealous for God as any of you are today" (Acts 22:3). Gamaliel was a Jewish rabbi, a Pharisee and teacher of the law, well respected for his learning and knowledge which he would have passed onto young Pharisees like Paul, or Saul as he was called before his conversion.

God uses Paul's education in his mission, but Paul doesn't rely on this education, he relies on the grace of God. He says, "For I am the least of the apostles and do not even deserve to be called an apostle, because I persecuted the church of God. But by the grace of God I am what I am, and His grace to me was not without effect. No, I worked harder than all of them—yet not I, but the grace of God that was with me" (1 Corinthians 15:9-10).

The point of this is your education may have directly led you to a specific career, as your schooling led from one thing to another chronologically and you built up qualifications step by step. Or your education may not have set you up for your career aspirations at all. There will have been choices you had to make along the way which will have impacted each stage of your education. This is not just about the subjects you studied, but what you actually learnt and enjoyed.

I really enjoyed the science subjects early on in my school career and did as well in them as in other subjects, and yet, when it came time to choose my A levels, I chose the humanities. Then at university I chose History before switching to English Literature which I really loved.

Sue's Education

At school Sue, recognised she was academic and a grafter. She says,

> *"I've always grafted, I would always do all my homework. I would always do what I was supposed to do. I wanted to understand things and I wanted to achieve academically. I wanted to do well at school. That's just the way I'm made up."*

She enjoyed biology and chemistry at school and after completing her A levels went to university and trained to become a Doctor.

David's Education

David, had a different experience at school. He loved Primary School where he learned about nature and grew his drawing ability. However, he struggled at Secondary school, being dyslexic[2] and discalculistic[3] as well as being mercilessly bullied. The teachers were on strike a lot of the time which meant there were no opportunities for extra-curricular support. He says,

> *"I left school, aged 16, feeling I was thick and really stupid. Thankfully I started a Youth Training Scheme (YTS) and it was the happiest day of my life. I left school behind and I went to work for this guy who was really great. I was paid to work outside building and creating stuff. I just love being outside. I never looked back and this was the start of learning my trade, my craft and my passion for working outside in all the seasons."*

When you consider your education include what you learnt in school and any formal education you had post school. Also think about the things you learnt outside of school. Were you involved in sport, music, drama, scouts or martial arts? Think in terms of topics of what you learned from your education and focus on the things you enjoyed or found useful; for example, you don't need to include everything you learned in science unless this is specific to your career aspirations and choices. However, to pursue a career in ecology you might find yourself recording all the geography, geology, chemistry and biology topics which were relevant or you might just record your qualification and grades.

There might be subjects you would have liked to have studied but were unable to for whatever reason. Any appealing subjects you haven't yet studied should be noted down later on your Interests branch. When you come to create your Vine, I suggest you don't make this a laborious process, just include what comes easily to mind.

Remember you're looking for clues about God's plan for your career. Often these clues are best found in the subjects you made an active decision to learn about, so this would include the subjects you specifically chose to study rather than those you were forced to study.

Activity 12: Your Education Branch

Make a note of anything of relevance about your education – these should be things you really enjoyed learning.

Note down your specific qualifications.

- What other things did you learn outside of your formal education?
- What grades or levels did you achieve in these areas?
- Was there anything specific you learnt?

Go back over your list and highlight or put a star against anything you enjoyed learning the most.

Prayer

Father God, thank You for my education.
As I review it now to plot out my Education branch remind me of anything I may have forgotten which is of relevance to me for my future career.

In Jesus name, Amen.

YOUR KNOWLEDGE

'The heart of the discerning acquires knowledge,
for the ears of the wise seek it out'.
(Proverbs 18:15)

Have you heard the proverb, *'a little knowledge is a dangerous thing'*? It was originally coined by Alexander Pope as *'a little learning is a dangerous thing'*.[4] I discovered just how true this was when I was visiting the paediatrician with my new-born son. I knew I wanted to make the most of this appointment and 'swotted up' on all the right medical terms for topics I wanted to discuss. At the time I had several friends who were medics, so I had become accustomed to the medical terms they bandied around. Halfway through the consultation the paediatrician asked me curiously, *"Do you have a medical background?"* No! I most certainly did not! I realised then how easy it would be to take a misstep for not having enough knowledge or from being misinformed.

We are exposed to a vast array of knowledge about all kinds of things from the infinite cosmos, to the tiny seeds which grow in the earth, to the way our brains work, to how chemicals form polymers and so on. So much of this knowledge is good, and God uses the knowledge we gain throughout our lives. In James 3:17 it says, 'the wisdom that comes from heaven is first of all pure; then peace-loving, considerate, submissive, full of mercy and good fruit, impartial and sincere'.

We live in a knowledge economy where knowledge is at our fingertips, easily accessible at the touch of a button or keypad, or even just asking Amazon's Alexa or Apple's Siri. And yet, we all have specific ways of interacting with knowledge, so it's not just what we know, but how we use what we know.

Howard Gardner, a psychologist, developed a theory of Multiple Intelligences[5] in the late 1980s suggesting that humans have a number of discrete intellectual capacities. From his research he identified 8 different components of Multiple Intelligence.

- **Bodily/Kinaesthetic** – Someone who is strong in bodily/kinaesthetic intelligence typically learns by doing. They will be well co-ordinated and good with their hands. They will understand about practical and physical objects and like movement, creating or touching things. Their knowledge will come from the practical, physical aspects of life.
- **Musical** – people with a strong musical intelligence will often be tuned into auditory features. They may have a good sense of rhythm, an ability to memorise songs and enjoy different sounds. They might be talented with musical instruments or be able to compose music. They may be humming or singing or tapping their feet all the time. Often, they will have music on in the background as they work.
- **Logical/Mathematical** – people with this intelligence will tend to be logical thinkers, enjoy numbers and order, and look for precision in chaos. They are likely to be good at maths and will tend to be objective in their outlook. They may see patterns everywhere and seek out correlations. They will learn by solving problems and experimenting.
- **Interpersonal** – those with interpersonal intelligence will often be found surrounded by people. They will have a keen sense of empathy

and be able to interpret verbal and non-verbal cues effectively. These people will learn and perform best when they are in group settings and interacting with people.

- **Intra-personal** – people with intrapersonal intelligence are very self-aware, intuitive and can be philosophical. They will tend to be independent learners who enjoy reflecting and are very in tune with their inner feelings and motives.
- **Linguistic** – someone with a strong linguistic intelligence likes words and is sensitive to their meanings. They may be an avid reader, or writer, good at learning other languages, and able to communicate effectively with words.
- **Spatial/Visual** – these people are able to visualise objects and have a good understanding of spatial awareness. They like maps, diagrams, graphs and charts. They may have a good sense of direction and be more observant than other people.
- **Naturalist** – someone with a high naturalist intelligence may feel an affinity with nature and the environment. They may have an understanding of animals or plants. They are likely to be inspired by nature and the outdoors and be knowledgeable about environmental issues.

As you look at these intelligences, what resonates with you? Which of these areas tends to drive your knowledge? Are you drawn to more than one area?

- Do you have a high level of interpersonal intellect? Then it is probable you will have a comprehensive knowledge of how people connect and interact.
- Are you someone who has a high musical intellect? You may find your knowledge is specific to this and you process information in a musical way. Are you always playing music?
- Are you strong in logical/mathematical intelligence? Do you look for patterns and connections? Are you a brilliant problem solver?
- Does your intelligence lie in the spatial/visual segment? Are you really knowledgeable about design?
- Do you have a high level of naturalist intelligence and know lots about flora and fauna?

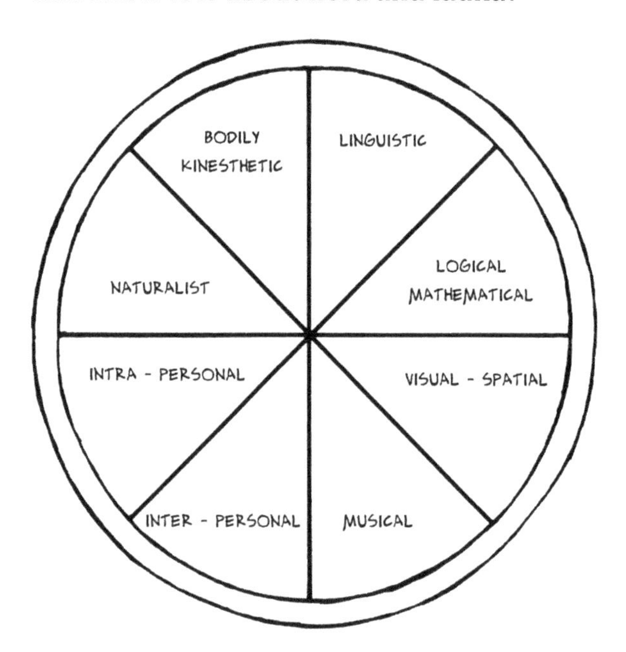

Wheel of Intelligence

Naturalist intelligence was added after Gardener's initial research. Some years later Gardner considered existentialist intelligence as a possible ninth intelligence to include a knowledge of the spiritual or moral, however he says this is still 'in limbo'[6]. Allegedly, people with this intelligence are able to see the 'bigger picture' and are comfortable conceptualising philosophical ideas about human existence and purpose. They might view the world through a religious or spiritual lens, but Gardner 'insisted that existential intelligence was not in and of itself a religious or spiritual or sacred capacity'. It is more about a propensity to ask big questions and ponder possible answers.

Using Gardner's Intelligences provides a very useful framework for sorting your knowledge, because it is intelligence driven rather than subject driven. From it, I realise I am strongly linguistic in the way I use my intelligence. I like to interpret things through words. I am also keenly interpersonal, liking to interact with people, as well as being intra-personal, being deeply reflective in the way I process information.

David's Knowledge

When I discussed Gardner's Intelligences with David, he could identify levels within the intelligences. From our earlier conversation, I knew David has very strong naturalistic, visual and spatial intelligence. However, he also suggested, *"I'm not musical, as in playing an instrument, but I think I am musical"* because he uses this intelligence in the way he relates to the world around him. He also talked about creativity and how many people view themselves as not creative and how he, *"Loves to bring out the artistic side of people and encourage their creativity."*

Each of the intelligences lend themselves to developing creativity! People with high linguistic intelligence like me, might write or speak for a living. Designers like David will create amazing spaces. People with high interpersonal intelligence might create places for people to interact.

As always, be wary of boxing yourself in. I had a client who consistently told me she wasn't good at maths and yet scored highly in the logical/mathematical sphere. It turns out that she is keenly logical and analytical despite not enjoying numbers, so the way she interpreted knowledge was in a logical and methodical manner.

Gardner's approach helps to get away from the traditional idea of knowledge you might have learned in school and helps you think about the knowledge you've gained in a broader context. There is so much knowledge you can gain from all the different jobs you've done. When you think about your knowledge, consider what you've learned from work, the courses you've attended and what you gained 'on-the-job'. Also, consider what knowledge you learned outside work, through volunteering or unpaid work, or just being curious about the world we live in.

Another word of caution: Beware the realised strength (Chapter Three: ABILITIES) of **'Curiosity'**. This strength means *'you are interested in everything, constantly seeking out new information and learning more'* so if this is a realised strength for you it's likely you will spend a long time in this section! As far as possible try to be circumspect and just note down key things. You can always take a highlighter to the ones which appeal to you most to explore them in more depth later on. For now, it is about being clear about your areas of knowledge, focusing on your personal expertise.

Activity 13: Your Knowledge Branch

- Which of Gardner's Intelligences resonate with you the most?

List them in order of preference based on what you know about yourself.

Quickly list under each intelligence your knowledge and expertise that fits in this area.

Reflect on other knowledge you have learned from work, courses attended and things you know from outside work.

Note these down under the relevant intelligences.

Prayer

Father God, thank You for all the knowledge You have given me. Please bring to mind anything You want me to add to my Knowledge branch at this time.

In Jesus name, Amen.

YOUR INTERESTS

'And now, dear brothers and sisters, one final thing. Fix your thoughts on what is true, and honourable, and right, and pure, and lovely, and admirable. Think about things that are excellent and worthy of praise'.

(Philippians 4:8 NLT)

God has made a vast universe, a beautiful world with so much to be discovered. There is much to be curious about. He has made each of us with unique interests and curiosities. It's exciting to be able to explore the areas which interest you. This is the time to let your mind wander, to let your thoughts flow!

- What interests you outside work?
- What are you curious about? These could be things you've dipped your toe in the water with, or you are saving to do later, but haven't quite got round to.
- What topics are you drawn to on television, or in the news, or in social media?
- What leisure activities do you enjoy doing? Sport, cooking, shopping, gardening ...?

Since the pandemic, there has been a big focus on our mental wellbeing. According to the charity Mind, one of the five ways to wellbeing, as researched and developed by the New Economics Foundation is 'continued learning through life'. This *'enhances self-esteem and encourages social interaction and a more active life'*[7]. Pursuing our interests is good for us!

What would you happily spend hours pursuing or learning about? These areas give us huge clues about the work and careers God has planned for us. That's not to say, you need to turn your hobby into a career (some people really don't want to do this) but being interested in the work you do makes a huge difference to your daily wellbeing. It could be you're interested in people and your work fulfils this interest or it could be you're fascinated by how our bodies work, or you love animals, or you're interested in patterns, music, or the outdoors. When you know what your interests are and can talk about them enthusiastically this will help bring alive a job application or help you come across as passionate and authentic in an interview.

Think through your day or week. What has stopped you in your tracks; what has distracted you, the topics you find yourself exploring or talking about? These could be at work or outside work. They could be full-blown hobbies or just small things which consistently attract your attention. Think about what type of magazine you would pull off a rack whilst waiting for a train, or what YouTube videos you find yourself continually watching, or the podcasts you regularly tune into, or the TV programmes you tend to watch. What do you do when you have a moment to yourself?

John L. Holland developed an interests classification test in the 1950s called the *Holland Occupational Themes*[8] which is still used today. It is designed to group people according to their suitability to six categories of occupation, based on personal likes and dislikes known as **RIASEC** markers - **Realistic, Investigative, Artistic, Social, Enterprising,** and **Conventional.** The idea is the things which interest you fall broadly into these six occupational areas which can be helpful when exploring career ideas.

- **R - Realistic** – someone who likes doing things. Their interests will include practical activities, such as mending items, building contraptions, operating machinery, or a love of mechanical objects. They might love to play sport and being outdoors, being physically active.

- **I - Investigative** – someone who likes abstract thinking. These people like solving complex problems and analysing data. They might love scientific research and finding new ways or working. They will often have several research projects on the go, either personal or professional.
- **A - Artistic** – someone who likes to create things. This could be creating art, or music, or writing or designing something. These people like to

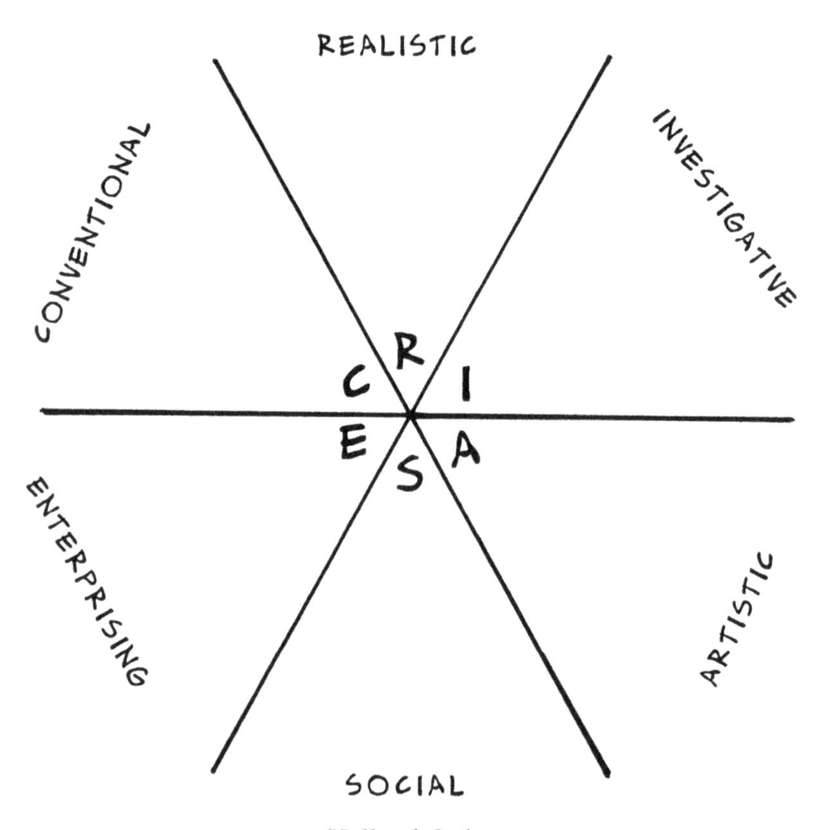

Holland Code

use their imagination and intuition to express themselves creatively. They are likely to have lots of creative projects, all at the same time.

- **S - Social** – someone who likes to be with other people. This could be helping other people, leading people, organising activities for other people, being part of social groups or teams. These people spend a lot of time with other people and love to communicate and empathise and co-operate with others.
- **E - Enterprising** – someone who likes to persuade. These people are often at the forefront of projects or activities. They love to galvanise other people to follow their lead. They can be adventurous whilst exploring options. They are likely to be happy to speak up and use their energy and drive to promote the things they feel passionate about.
- **C - Conventional** – someone who likes to be organised. These people like detail, processes and procedures where they can operate in methodical and conscientious manner. They love making sure everything is in the right place, whilst being neat and orderly, and are happy to take responsibility for this.

Are you struggling to think of your interests? Draw a RAISEC grid and jot down your ideas in the relevant segments to build up a picture of where your interests lie. What are the activities you like to do which fall into each of these areas? Remember God didn't design you to fit in a box or a grid, so don't try to squeeze yourself into one either. It's likely your interests will fall across more than one of these RIASEC markers to a larger or smaller degree.

Activity 14: Your Interest Branch

Let your mind flow!

- What interests you?

Note down headings, topics or areas of interest on some yellow stickies or cards.

Don't worry about focussing on details at this moment, you're looking for clues which you can come back to later.

Organise your interests under relevant themes, using the Holland Code, Realistic, Investigative, Artistic, Social, Enterprising, Conventional or your own headings.

Put to one side anything you consider a hobby, or a 'love to do' but you wouldn't want to do as a job.

List your interests in order of preference depending on what is most appealing to you using a scale of 1-5, where 1 is not appealing and 5 is really appealing.

Prayer

Father God, thank You so much for the
many things which interest me.
Give me discernment as I explore them
on my Interest branch.

In Jesus name, Amen.

YOUR COMPASSION

'The Lord is gracious and compassionate, slow to anger and rich in love. The Lord is good to all; He has compassion on all He has made'.

(Psalm 145:8-9)

So many times in the Bible we read about God's compassion. As Psalm 145 above says, 'He is compassionate' and 'He has compassion on all He has made'. Time and time again Jesus responds when He is moved by compassion to help people, to restore them, to heal them, to draw them into His kingdom. 'Jesus called His disciples to Him and said, "I have compassion for these people; they have already been with me three days and have nothing to eat. I do not want to send them away hungry, or they may collapse on the way" (Matthew 15:32).

Jesus, moved by compassion, attended to their needs, in this case feeding 4000 men plus the women and children! In Luke 7 we read how Jesus encounters a widow whose only son has died. 'When the Lord saw her, His heart overflowed with compassion. "Don't cry!" He said' (Luke 7:13 NTL). His heart overflowed with compassion, or "His heart went out to her" (NIV) or "His heart broke" (MSG). This is how you know the things for which you have compassion; your heart breaks, your compassion overflows, your heart goes out to the person or the situation.

Since we are made in the image of God (Genesis 1:27) and we know God is compassionate, it makes sense that we are driven by compassion as well.

According to the Cambridge Dictionary the meaning of compassion is 'a strong feeling or sympathy and sadness for the suffering or bad luck of others and a wish to help them.'[9] Compassion combines your feelings with action. It is when you are moved enough by something to take action, to want to make a difference. The etymology, or origin, of 'compassion' is from the Latin, 'com-passio' meaning 'co-suffering'[10] being sensitive to the suffering of others.

Sometimes when we look around us, or read or watch the news, we can be overwhelmed by the needs of our world. Just as God has made each of us different and unique, so He has given each of us a bit of his creation, earthly and spiritual, to care deeply about, to ache to do something to help or change. It could be people who are lost, single mothers, homelessness, persecuted Christians, debt, people in prison, slavery, trafficked people, mental health, the voiceless, the broken, the planet.

What do you care about? When you look at the world around you what touches you? What causes a lurch in your heart? What do you long to change? Sometimes, it might be areas which frustrate you, or deeply annoy you, or you feel a righteous anger about, as Jesus felt a righteous anger when he cleared the Temple of money lenders, or from loan sharks as it says in The Message version.

'Jesus put together a whip out of strips of leather and chased them out of the Temple, stampeding the sheep and cattle, upending the tables of the loan sharks, spilling coins left and right. He told the dove merchants, "Get your things out of here! Stop turning my Father's house into a shopping mall!" This is when his disciples remembered the Scripture, "Zeal for your house consumes me" (John 2:15-17 MSG).

Zeal is a great word! This sentence is taken from Psalm 69:9 with zeal translated as passion in the New Living Translation. 'Passion for your house has consumed me, and the insults of those who insult you have fallen on me' (Psalm 69:9 NLT).

Passion is 'a powerful emotion or its expression, especially the emotion of love, anger, or hate.'[11] It can be related to your emotions and also your interests. Some items on your list of interests could be areas you are passionate about. Your passions can drive your compassions! What fills you with zeal? What fills you with passion?

Jesus, full of passion and compassion, cleared the Temple so it could be restored to a house of prayer, returned to its rightful and intended use. 'And as He taught them, He said, "Is it not written: 'My house will be called a house of prayer for all nations'? But you have made it a' den of robbers'" (Mark 11:17).

Is your compassion driven by righteous anger and frustration, as much as by sadness for other people or situations? Knowing what issues resonate with your compassion can give you clues about God's plan for your career.

Jane's Compassion

Jane, an emotional health and wellbeing consultant for schools, was motivated by wanting to help the lost. She started her career as a teacher, before moving to education consulting where she has worked for the last 20 years, spending the last few providing mental health first aid training to teachers and school administrators. Coming to the end of her professional career, spending less time at work and with more time on her hands, she was considering doing some volunteering. She wanted to give back to the community, but she wasn't sure what that should be. In 2020, as we went into lockdown, she was working 2 days a week delivering Youth Mental Health First Aid training for teachers, which she really enjoyed.

At the same time, she was listening to the daily prayer devotional, Lectio 365[12] and says,

> *"I really enjoyed doing that every morning, and gradually building up my knowledge of the Bible and seeing the value in those little 10-minute chunks dipping into the Bible. One morning, during the closing prayer on Lectio, I experienced a strong message for me that felt absolutely right. The closing prayer starts, 'Father help me to live this day to the full ... and I thought, 'yes that's fine, that's a good start to the day.' Then "Jesus, help me to give myself away to others, being kind to everyone I meet" ... and I thought yes, generally I try to do that'. But the next line really resonated and really felt like a message for me. It was "Spirit help me to love the lost" ... and I thought 'this is God speaking to me, because this isn't something I do. I can do those other things, but how do I really love the lost? I thought 'well, during my mental health training, I talk about young people, but I'm not actually actively doing and loving the lost'.*
>
> *Then I had a moment where I just thought, 'maybe I could do something like Childline'?[13] I hadn't thought about it before. But it came through part of the closing prayer. I felt 'this is what I must do. It complements the training I do, talking about young people who are in need and who are lost. It's something I can actually do, and I've got the time'. I was aware of my physical limitations due*

to having Multiple Sclerosis (MS)[14] and when I thought about Childline, I realised my MS would not hinder me. I think God was also at work helping me to turn a weakness into something positive. Helping others certainly helps me not to feel too sorry for myself!"

Jane went on to train as a volunteer and regularly volunteers as a Childline counsellor. It wasn't all plain sailing, and you can read more in the section under God's Revelations.

Sheralyn's Compassion

Sheralyn, is driven by her compassion for survivors of modern slavery. She says,

"Wouldn't it be Woofterful® if dog owners could leave their dog somewhere safe and secure with high quality care in a nurturing and truly dog focused environment, whilst also providing training and supporting survivors of modern-day slavery?"

Her vision for Woofterful® Doggy Daycare is to provide a practical way to give dogs attention throughout the day, whilst also allowing dogs to provide natural companionship and emotional support to those who have experienced trauma. Sheralyn will be employing and training survivors of modern slavery through this social enterprise.

David's Compassion

David has compassion for disadvantaged people who have experienced discouragement in their lives. He says,

"A big part of my life now is encouraging people, helping people who are dyslexic who may think they are stupid. These people tend to find me; and I'm able to help them and bring out the best in them."

When I prayed about my compassions[15] – I wrote down the things that came to mind as a stream of consciousness. These are things I really care about, things which move me to action. You'll notice it's all a bit jumbled as my thoughts progressed and I wrote it as I prayed.

- Seekers – sharing my faith.
- Young 'new' Christians.
- People with depression.
- Identity – people who are lost and don't know who they are (in Christ).
- Animals – cats, dogs, horses, compassion – rescue.
- Hearing/reading stories of people who have been saved and are living God's purpose for their lives.
- I feel frustrated when people believe a lie about themselves instead of the truth (which is what God thinks of them).
- Healing – miracles, physical, spiritual and mental.
- People being baptised into the body of Christ.
- People who are lost because they don't know their loving Father.
- Adoption – reunited families.
- Mental health – depression, anxiety, fear.
- Helping people grow closer to Jesus and seeing the difference this makes to their lives.

- Helping people who feel stuck in some way – hearing stories about how they have become unstuck.
- Family, friends, helping people who are in trouble.
- Encouraging people to see the positives.
- People helping me in times of need.
- Praying for people and situations and seeing results.
- Being a Christian at work and how to 'live' this.
- Seeing people and situations through God's eyes.
- People who are finding life tough.
- Reconciliation – brings tears to my eyes.
- Restored families.
- Renewing the mind.

It is very personal to me. These are the groups of people or situations for whom I feel compassion. This list gave me a starting point for exploring my compassion and passion. I offer it to you as an example. Not everything went on my Vine of Curiosity, this was just the starting point, before I began to prune the list and choose which items should go on my Compassion branch.

What stirs your compassion?

- What do you feel passionate about?
- What are the needs you have been most responsive to in the past?
- What activities are you already involved in?
- Are you volunteering in areas you feel passionate about already?

There are so many 'causes' in the world that sometimes understanding which ones tug on your heart can be a bit overwhelming, so start small. Ask God to remind you of the time you felt sad about a homeless person, or when your heart went out to a single mother who was struggling in the local supermarket, or when you felt angry about the way refugees are treated, or your feelings of frustration about the way our planet is being abused. These are all clues about your compassion.

Activity 15: Your Compassion Branch

Start with prayer – ask God to reveal to you everything which causes compassion to rise up in you.

Then list them as a stream of consciousness.

Keep writing until you run out of ideas.

Take a break

Go back over your list and grade them according to how compassionate, or passionate you feel.

Use grade ...

A - for things you feel really compassionate about, things you find dwell in your mind.

B - for things you feel moderately compassionate about.

C - for things which move you but don't cause you sleepless nights.

You may find there are some things you want to grade A*.

Prayer

Father God, I know Your heart beats with compassion. Fill my heart with Your compassion and let Your Holy Spirit guide me as I list the things which fill me with passion and compassion.

In Jesus name, Amen.

YOUR INNER WISDOM

'Yet You desired faithfulness even in the womb,
You taught me wisdom in that secret place'.
(Psalm 51:6)

Your inner wisdom? What's this? I hear you ask. Your inner wisdom is the personal knowledge stored in the secret part of you; what you know about yourself in your heart but not necessarily in your head. This is not the same as your intuition, your compassion, or your inner voice. This is more about the things you 'know' you are meant to do in your life or career. You can almost feel them 'in your gut' as Lynne Lee speaks about in her *Discover Your Life Purpose course*[16]. These are thoughts planted deep in you which God is longing to help you unearth. When He was creating your inmost being, He planted these ideas in you, ready for you to act on them.

It's different for all of us. When I prayed about my inner wisdom what came to mind included 'write a book,' 'have a family,' 'lead home groups', and 'be a coach'. These are areas I didn't really need anyone else to tell me I was meant to be doing or accomplishing in my life; I just knew them in my heart!

These things went onto my Vine of Curiosity and gradually God has revealed more about the 'where' and the 'how' for each one.

I have always 'known' I was meant to write a book, but I didn't know what the book would be about. I'd even signed up for a Creative Writing course trying to pursue this inner idea. When I was seeking God deeply about His purpose for my life, He reminded me about the book, and this time there was more information – a book on God's plan for our careers – combining my vision for Christian career coaching with writing a book. How Great is God! My heart surged with excitement and joy as what I knew all along in my 'inner wisdom' was being fulfilled.

Natasha's Inner Wisdom

Natasha, a consultant and founder of *Impact People and Change* describes her cultural exchange trip to Uganda as something she *"always knew she was meant to do."* I interviewed her to find out a bit more. She said,

> *"I've always kind of known I was made for something special in the work I was going to do. I can't describe it as anything other than just having a feeling about, or a real desire to give back or make a difference to other people's lives. I've been really fortunate and been able to do this in a number of different ways throughout my career. And it felt like Uganda was it. I'm not professing to be a missionary; there are lots of other people who go and do international development work at a much bigger scale than me.*
>
> *For me, it had to be at the right time in my life as well, at a point where I felt I had invested a lot in my career. I'd been made redundant in 2017 and took a job working in consultancy in local government. I really enjoyed the senior leadership development work but I felt disconnected to my purpose. I didn't feel as though I was really making a direct impact on disadvantaged people in the community. I also experienced some personal challenges in 2018 and the cumulation of events took me to the cusp of burnout. I felt it was a good time to step away, when I had no ties, and do*

something to reconnect with my purpose. I felt a real pull, a real kind of calling to actually reconnect with this purpose and to do something really meaningful.

Despite the challenges I faced in 2018, something pulled me to put in an application for an opportunity with International Citizens Service (ICS).[17] *It involved working overseas on a community development project, leading a team of volunteers on a blended cultural exchange programme delivering sexual health education and entrepreneurship. There was dual purpose to the programme - to do development work, and for it to be a cultural exchange programme as the volunteer team were from both UK and Uganda.*

I remember getting to the interview in London after I'd had a difficult day the day before, I felt quite down and got close to thinking I'll just not bother here. Yet there was something pulling me and getting me on that train in the morning and saying, "You know what, get yourself to London, see what it's all about, really give it everything." And I did absolutely. I gave it everything in the interview and it was a hard interview. About a week later, I found out I'd been successful, and felt a huge, warmth, and a real excitement around me. Receiving the offer email, and suddenly there was hope, direction, and a confirmation; "Yes, this is what I was meant to do." I desperately wanted it to be Uganda, rather than Nepal. It was one of the two. I found out it was Uganda two or three weeks later. My Mum and I prayed for Uganda, I remember being quite emotional at the time, and feeling really responsible, not just privileged to have the opportunity, but it felt like it was my duty - my calling.

It was an amazingly restorative experience for me; I had connected with my purpose. I met friends and family with whom I am still linked with today, people I can call my family. I also had a moment in the village where I felt God's presence. I can close my eyes and visualise it. I was in the village, children were around me. I was about 100 yards from the house and I was running. I was noticeably different to others in the village and everyone knew who I was. At that moment, I just felt a huge presence of God's Spirit. The trip gave me so much more than I ever thought I would get and I will forever be grateful. It's shaped the work I've chosen to do ever since."

What a fabulous story! How amazing that Natasha felt she's always known she would do something special like this; God had planted this wisdom in her. When the time was right, she acted on it and God met her in such a strong and vivid way. How wonderful God should use this to restore her sense of purpose in her career and direct her steps from this experience to what she is doing now;

"Partnering with mission driven organisations and making a difference in the direct work that I do. Even if I'm quite far removed from the frontline, and I'm working with the senior leader, I need to make a difference for that person. They can then make a difference to the people in their business and the communities they're supporting."

What is your 'inner wisdom' telling you?

This might need some discernment and prayer! You might need to ask God specifically if there is anything He wants you to put on this branch.

Activity 16: What's in Your Inner wisdom?

Start with prayer – ask God to reveal what He has planted in your inner wisdom, when He knit you together in your mother's womb.

Write these things down – you should feel a surge of recognition or excitement, small or large, a sense of 'rightness' as you write!

Don't worry if your list is short, it's the content which is of value not the quantity.

Prayer

Father God, thank You for the things you planted in my inner wisdom as You knit me together in my mothers' womb. Prompt me now as I write them down.

In Jesus name, Amen.

YOUR REVELATIONS FROM GOD

'If people can't see what God is doing, they stumble all over themselves; But when they attend to what He reveals, they are most blessed'.

(Proverbs 29:18 MSG)

Did you know that God wants to reveal His thoughts about your career to you? In my experience His specific revelations are very personal and may include any of the following:

- Specific prophecies spoken over you
- Bible verses which are significant for you
- Words of wisdom from other Christians
- Suggestions which come from prayer times
- Ideas sparked by exploring God's amazing creation.

Learning to hear how God is speaking to you about your career, and of course every aspect of life, is invaluable and I highly recommend you make this a priority.

Revelation can be the light bulb moment when you're reading your Bible and suddenly something 'clicks' and you understand what the passage is about. It feels special and significant as if God is speaking directly to you. It's when God deepens your understanding by revealing the scriptures to you through the Holy Spirit in a way which is deeply personal.

This is the main way God reveals things to me; how He shines a light on my path (Psalm 119:105). There have been significant verses at specific times in my life and career which have had particular meaning for me. The first was, 'Neither do people light a lamp and put it under a bowl. Instead they put it on its stand, and it gives light to everyone in the house' (Matthew 5:15).

Reading this impacted me deeply when I was seeking Jesus, it was like a light bulb moment. Pun intended! It was as if God was saying to me, if you believe in me, in Jesus, don't hide it, but join with other believers and let your lights shine together for other people to see. Why indeed would anyone light a light and then hide it away? God knew I needed a prompt to step out and join with other believers.

He still uses this verse today to remind me not to hide my light of faith, but to join with other Christians to let my light be seen by other people. God continues to shine a light on my path through words I read in the Bible. You'll no doubt have noted the many scriptural references in this book – this is no accident!

The next passage God revealed to me was Acts 2:42-47, entitled 'The fellowship of the believers' in my NIV Bible. The last verse particularly resonates for me, 'And the Lord added to their number daily those who were being saved' (Acts 2:47b). I felt it was through the prayers of the fellowship of believers at the Church I joined, that God 'added me to their number'. It warms my heart to be part of this fellowship now.

This leads me to two other ways God reveals things to us; through fellowship with other believers and through prayer.

Sometimes God reveals Himself through other believers. Someone might say something which connects with you and is related to something you are considering or pondering at the time, although unbeknown to the other person.

God also reveals Himself through prayer. During the

pandemic, I committed to pray for one hour once a week, along with other members of my Church. I devised a format for this which included worship, confession, reading and meditating on a Bible passage and then praying for myself, my family, my church family, my local region, the nation, the world and then giving thanks to God at the end. The Bible passage one day was Matthew 9:36, Jesus again showing compassion. 'When He saw the crowds, He had compassion on them, because they were harassed and helpless, like sheep without a shepherd. Then He said to His disciples, "The harvest is plentiful, but the workers are few."' (Matthew 9:36-37).

I was struck by the idea of people *'harassed and helpless, like sheep without a shepherd'* especially during the early days of the pandemic in 2020. Then *'the harvest of believers was plentiful and yet the workers few'*. I prayed about my own insufficiency, my own fears, my sense that God wanted to use my career coaching talents for His purposes, especially for other members of the body of Christ. I wanted to be obedient and yet I was letting fear get in the way. After pouring out my prayer to God, I happened to glance at my desk calendar, which I get sent by United Christian Broadcasters (UCB)[18] every year, and the verse for that month was: 'RISE UP ... TAKE COURAGE AND DO IT' (Ezra 10:4 their capitals).

This was the answer I needed. God said take courage and do it! This is what he wanted me to do. I look at my calendar on most days, but until that specific prayer time this verse had not resonated with me at all. God revealed what He wanted me to do through my prayer, and this also gave me the confidence boost I needed.

God also reveals Himself through creation, and this may be the way He shows His plans to you. 'For ever since the world was created, people have seen the earth and sky. Through everything God made, they can clearly see His invisible qualities—His eternal power and divine nature. So they have no excuse for not knowing God' (Romans 1:20 NLT).

You may find things make sense to you through nature, when a spiritual truth becomes apparent through a physical example, or through a conversation with someone, or even through circumstances which may appear co-incidental but are in fact God speaking to you. In his book, *How to Hear God – A Simple Guide for Normal People,* Pete Greig describes how we can discern 'the voice of God in the whole of life, not just in religious contexts, but also in the actualities of community, creation and culture.'[19]

David's Revelations

I asked David, whether he had received any prophecies he was willing to share. When he was a young man, he went on a youth retreat with the church he attended.

> *"I was in a Pentecostal church where the freedom of worship and freedom of the Holy Spirit would really flow and this guy called Andy prophesied over me. He prophesied that I would be a leading light in my city. I remember thinking, 'That's a bit weird' since at the time I wasn't doing anything in particular. Looking back, it was a very powerful prophecy, which I believed but found really hard to accept, since it wasn't the classic, 'You're going to become a minister or whatever'. They always say with prophesy to hold it, but don't grip it. Sometimes I come back and think, 'Why would God say that?' In my heart there's an affirmation around this prophecy but also a kind of a natural striving inside around this prophecy. Part of what I do now, is so much*

about how I share my faith with people through my business. It's about the influence I have in my local area, where I'm very visible and people know I'm a Christian, so I live it out in the public arena. My conviction in living out my faith is more powerful than building my career. So, if you asked me 'What's my career? I'd say 'My career is my faith' because the two are so entwined. I can't separate the two because the position I'm able to have in the community and in the building community, through my business, lets me go into places I wouldn't otherwise be able to go to share my faith."

Jane's Revelations

Jane, who volunteers for Childline, says training to become a Childline counsellor was very challenging. She explains,

"I used to get really anxious and nervous about it, because it was so out of my comfort zone. Although I've been a teacher, I've never done counselling. This is a whole new area with new skills, but I didn't feel on my own. I never doubted, I never wanted to give up. I felt I had God with me, by my side, all the way through this, even when my mentor sessions didn't go particularly well. I had to do four sessions whereas most people only did two! There were many challenges along the way; I found it difficult to listen to the supervisor; follow the screen and learn the way you have to actually speak to the young people. It felt like spinning plates. I hadn't had those feelings of such anxiety and nerves since I did my driving test or the day of exams, but in some ways, it's been exhilarating to go through.

I carried on with Lectio 365, and I used to keep a diary and write little notes. I've looked back at them, to see

what I was writing down. Basically, I've written Bible verses that resonated with me at the time! Isaiah 41:13, "For I am the Lord your God, who takes hold of your right hand and says to you, Do not fear I will help you," which I wrote down twice. It really saved me because it connected with how I was feeling at that time. Psalm 16:8, "I keep my eyes always on the Lord. With Him at my right hand, I shall not be shaken". Once when I was on a shift, 2 Corinthians 1:4, 'God who comforts us all in our troubles, so that we can comfort those in any trouble with the comfort we ourselves receive from God'. I felt it was relevant when I'm talking to the young people."

Jane also describes God's revelation through other people.

"I had a real wobble around the time of Covid-19. There was a case at the base and so we couldn't go in. They had to change all the regulations and clean everything down. When it opened again, I was really keen to go back, but my husband said, "Jane, I don't think you should go in. I think you should wait till you've had your vaccination". This was pre-vaccinations. I was very frustrated because I really wanted to continue and I thought, "If I stop now, I'm going to lose confidence and I'm not going to want to go back in again.' I knew my husband was concerned because of my MS and was speaking out of love for me and his desire to protect me. Then I went for a walk with my friend who's quite a risk taker; she's a person who will go for it. I thought, "She's going to say to me, "Go on Jane it's fine. Don't worry about your husband, he's just being overprotective.

But she didn't. She said, "No, that makes sense. It's just a few weeks wait for the vaccination." I felt God was talking to me through my friend because I was surprised and I thought she would say, "You'll be fine". I realised this was two people who care about me who've said the same thing, and God was speaking to me through them."

Now it is your turn!

What has God told you or revealed to you? There might be specific Bible verses He has given you. There might be words of wisdom given to you from another believer, through the Holy Spirit. You might have had word of prophecy given to you. My advice here is to rest in God and see what He brings to mind! Take your time over this and be prepared to come back to it a few times.

Activity 17:
Your Revelations From God.

Start with prayer and ask God to remind you of things He has specifically revealed to you.

- Are there specific Bible verses or passages that God has revealed to you?
- Are there things another believer said to you which touched you deeply?
- Have you had words of prophecy prayed over you? What were they?
- Are there particular events or circumstances where God has revealed things to you?

Make a note of these revelations.

Prayer

Father God, thank You for the things You have revealed to me about my career. Bring them to mind again now.

In Jesus name, Amen.

REFLECTION ACTIVITY:
YOUR VINE OF CURIOSITY

'I am the true vine, and my Father is the gardener.
He cuts off every branch in me that bears no fruit, while every branch that does bear fruit He prunes
so that it will be even more fruitful.'

(John 15:1-2)

Throughout this chapter you will have gathered lots of ideas of the things you are curious about. Now it is time to create your own Vine of Curiosity by going back through each area prayerfully pruning so you are left with something manageable.

As you go back through the information you have gathered in each section use a highlighter or sticky stars or labels to prayerfully mark the key things which stand out for you.

You could use the following scale to help your pruning process.

- A - this is really important for me, I'm really drawn to it.
- B - this is somewhat important for me.
- C - I'm interested but don't feel prompted to take it further.
- D - this is part of who I am but it is time to let this go.

Take a large sheet of A4 or some flip chart paper and some coloured pens. Write JESUS at the bottom of the page where the roots of the vine would be. Use the picture at the start of the chapter as a guide.

Next, draw branches for each different area; education, knowledge, interests, compassion, inner wisdom and revelation.

Then, populate the drawing with words or pictures that you have highlighted or starred as you complete each branch.

Use different coloured pens for each branch to help make your vine more dynamic.

Don't be surprised if some branches have more on them than others.

Then, take a break! Let this settle for a day or two.

Add a bit more as you review what you've done, as God prompts you.

As you progress through the diagram in prayer you may find you decide to cut off or prune things and cast them away, so you are left with things which will prove to be fruitful in your career.

Prayer

Father God, thank You for the curiosity You have given me. Prompt me and remind me of things relevant to me for each of the branches as I create my Vine of Curiosity.

In Jesus name, Amen.

GRACE

Gifts
Relationships
Abilities
Curiosities
Experiences

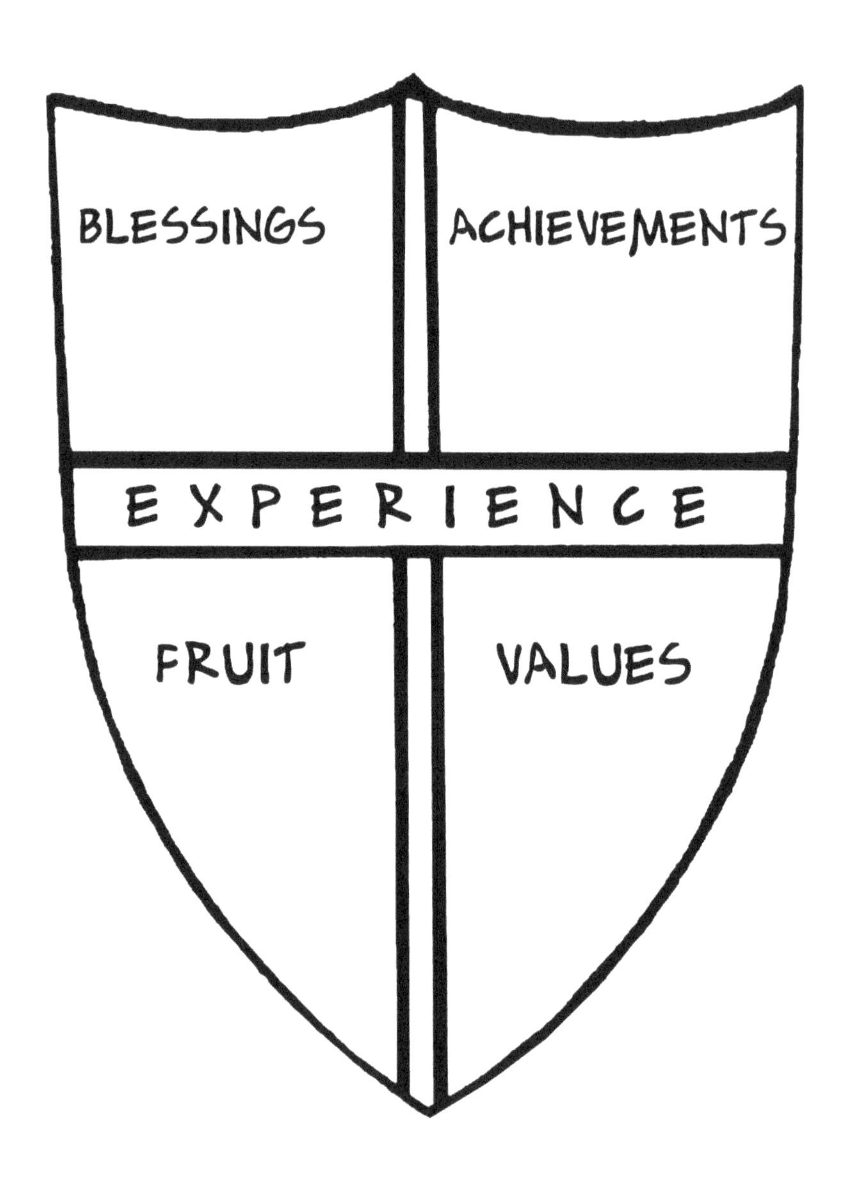
BLESSINGS
ACHIEVEMENTS
EXPERIENCE
FRUIT
VALUES

Chapter Five: EXPERIENCES

'And we know that in all things God works for the good of those who love Him, who have been called according to His purpose'.

(Romans 8:28)

Søren Kierkegaard, the Christian philosopher wrote, 'Life can only be understood backwards; but it must be lived forwards.'[1] This quote comes from Volume IV of his journals, written around 1843. Kierkegaard suggests we can only really understand our lives by looking back on things we've already done.

Hindsight is a wonderful thing. We can all learn from the good and the bad events which happen in our lives. We are shaped by them all, and by our response to them. God wastes nothing and He is always making good from the bad, using all your life to create the person He intends you to be.

When you look back you can see the clues God has given you for your future and unearth the treasure He has left to guide you on your **Career Journey**. We all have stories from our career journeys which have impacted on what we do next, but it's knowing where to look. The Message version of Galatians 6:4-5 says, 'Make a careful exploration of who you are and the work you have been given, and then sink yourself into that. Don't be impressed with yourself. Don't compare yourself with others. Each of you must take responsibility for doing the creative best you can with your own life'.

As you begin this careful exploration of your career, firstly look at the big picture and review your career journey to date. Then you can focus on your **Achievements**, the satisfying times as well as the difficult times when you had to dig deep to overcome them and the lessons you learned. Armed with these stories you will be able to identify the **Fruit** in your career. The idea of bearing fruit in your career encompasses not just what you do or have done, but also how you do it and how your character displays spiritual fruit. You will also consider the **Blessings** God has provided in your career, helping you to lift your gaze to Him and identify how He is at work in and through your career. Finally, you will uncover the **Values** that are unique to you. Knowing, understanding and articulating your values is arguably the most important aspect of flourishing in your career because this is how you feel most authentic and true to yourself and who God has made you to be.

Prayer

Father God, as I explore my experience, both
in life and work, help me reflect on the themes
and lessons You want me to take forward.

In Jesus name, Amen.

YOUR CAREER JOURNEY

'Like an open book, You watched me grow from conception to birth; all the stages of my life were spread out before You. The days of my life all prepared before I'd even lived one day'.

(Psalm 139:15-16 MSG)

I really enjoy walking alongside people as they talk me through their career journey. There are always highs and lows, peaks and troughs, times of change, questionable decisions, times of learning and possibly times of waiting. You can learn so much about your character, skills, values, strengths and career motivations by reviewing your career journey.

Let's have a look at Joseph's career journey.

Joseph is a key character in the Bible whose journey sets him up for what was to come next. His story started with a dream (see Chapter One: GIFTS) and then this dream was derailed by what happened over the next few years. He was captured and enslaved, wrongly accused and imprisoned before being released and appointed by Pharaoh to govern Egypt. His story had highs and lows as God equipped him for his long-term career (Genesis 37-47).

Just imagine what Joseph's career journey would look like. He had a great childhood as the favoured son of his father singled out with an '*ornamented robe*' (Genesis 37:3 NIV 1984). As a teenager he has two unusual and vivid dreams and instead of seeking wise counsel he chooses to share them with his brothers. The consequences are huge. His brothers already despise him, because he is the favoured son, and when he shares his dreams of prosperity, they become extremely jealous, sell him to slave traders and he is trafficked to Egypt. This must have been very distressing for him and an extremely difficult time. He went from favoured son, to dejected slave. 'They bruised his feet with shackles, his neck was put in irons' (Psalm 105:18).

In Egypt, he is bought by Potiphar, captain of Pharaoh's guard, and is entrusted with the care of managing everything in Potiphar's estate. This was a time of flourishing for Joseph. However, he catches the eye of Potiphar's wife who tries to tempt him away from his work to sleep with her. Joseph resists, but she falsely accuses him of molesting her and he is imprisoned. Joseph clung to his integrity, but still ended up in prison because of Potiphar's wife's actions.

There are times in our careers where we are challenged to step into areas which are not right for us, when our egos are massaged, when shortcuts are offered. There are also times when we clash with other people, usually senior to us which

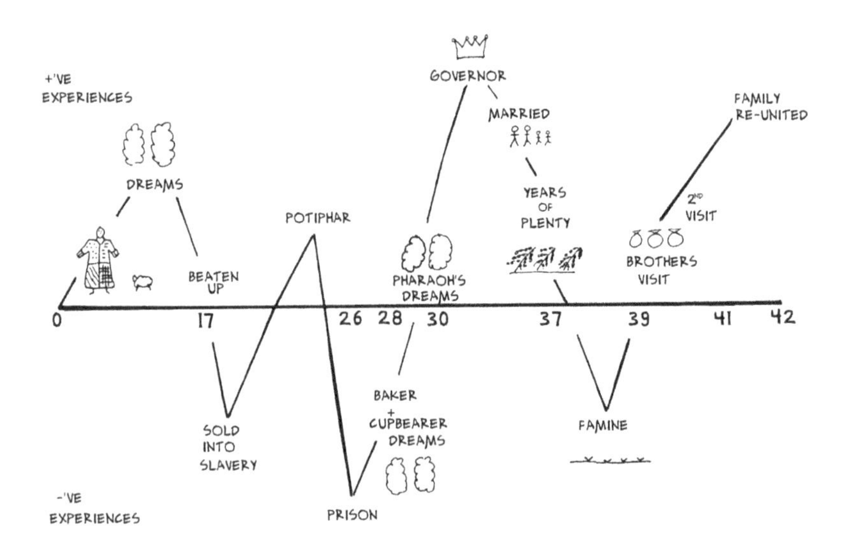

Joseph's Career Journey

causes stress and dissatisfaction. There may also be times when we are mistreated as Joseph was.

However, he is still able to use his skills. God's favour is on him and he is put in charge of all the prisoners. Pharaoh's cupbearer and bread-maker are also in prison. They both have strange dreams which through God's gifting Joseph is able to interpret. They are released from prison and their dreams come true. Despite this Joseph is left to languish in the prison for another two years. He has the skills as well as God's favour, but still has to endure a time of waiting and learning before being released. Finally, he is freed, when Pharaoh seeks interpretations for dreams he has had. Through God's divine revelation, Joseph is able to interpret Pharaoh's dreams and is offered the job of Governor.

As a result, he navigates the country through a time of preparation for severe famine. His career hits a highpoint with this immense achievement.

Imagine chatting with Joseph and asking him, with the benefit of hindsight, what patterns or themes could he see in his career journey?

- There's the theme of dreams. Dreams he received from God and other people's dreams he interpreted.
- There's a pattern of working hard and having God's favour, despite the circumstances.
- There's a time of injustice when he is wrongly accused and imprisoned.
- There's a time of waiting.

How many of these themes resonate with you? Have you had to wait for something in your career? Have you had a difficult boss or been unjustly accused? Has someone else taken the credit for your good work? What did you learn from these times?

What do you think Joseph would say if you asked him what he had learnt by looking back over his timeline? We know from what he says to his brothers when they are reunited, "You intended to harm me, but God intended it for good to accomplish what is now being done, the saving of many lives" (Genesis 50:20).

Reading Joseph's perspective on his difficult career, it's amazing to see how God was preparing him for his eventual role as Governor. God was working His purposes out through Joseph's life and He will be doing the same in your life. As a Christian, you can know God is at work in your career despite your circumstances.

Dewi's Experience

I spoke with Dewi, Managing Director of *Silverlock Tenders* and asked him, "When you look back over your career, how did God prepare you for each stage?" He commented,

> *"I wasn't aware that He was preparing me. But looking back at various points it's interesting because I can see things I wasn't enjoying in that season which I'm now using an awful lot."*

After university, Dewi spent 21 years working for the Civil Service in the Department of Trade and Industry which offered him a range of different opportunities and experiences. He then started his own business, *Silverlock Tenders,* a tender and bid writing company, helping small and medium sized businesses and charities to win contracts and get funding.

Looking back over his career, Dewi can see themes and patterns which led him to what he is doing now. The first was his understanding of businesses and how they work. He says,

> *"I wasn't particularly seeking a specific work area, but in pursuing my career over ten different posts I discovered I really enjoyed working with a wide range of small businesses from construction to film, advising them on grant funding and appraising grant applications. Working alongside these companies gave me a love for small and medium sized enterprises (SMEs) and an understanding of their values as I became 'business savvy'. This has helped me enormously in running my own business, building up a good rapport with clients, understanding how businesses work, including pricing and invoicing, as well as building a good reputation."*

His second theme is an understanding of grants and funding. One of the roles he had in the Civil Service was administering European funding, which he says he didn't particularly enjoy, commenting,

> *"The term conjures up the myriad of bureaucratic compliance rules and regulations which I had to deal with. However, it proved invaluable now as my work is all about helping businesses, charities and local authorities navigate the complexities of public funding using an understanding of complex rules and regulations so they can gain funding and win tenders through my company."*

Dewi knows what the public sector buyers want and his background knowledge is extremely beneficial in helping business and charities submit tenders to access funding.

His third theme is knowing how to write well. One job he had involved writing for senior government ministers, including the Deputy Prime Minister, on Department of Trade and Industry issues. He says,

"This honed my writing skills so I could convey information succinctly, and accurately in a way which could be easily understood. Looking back, this is invaluable in writing tenders. Although, I now employ associate writers, my understanding of good writing, means my key phrase of advice for anybody bidding for funding or a tender is, "Make it easy for the buyer to choose you."

With the benefit of hindsight, Dewi can cite examples of how his career experiences working alongside businesses, dealing with European funding and writing for government ministers have honed him for his current role. He can see how these threads have led to the work he now does.

Dewi also spoke of a time when he was approached by someone who was very complimentary about his skills and abilities, with a suggestion to run an associates referral business. His mentor advised him not to pursue this opportunity, but Dewi disregarded this. Looking back, he says,

> *"I spent three months pondering changing careers instead of pursuing what I already had, because somebody was very glowing about my skills. I learned a lot of lessons about getting good business advisors and listening to what they say; being open to them and not pushing back against their advice."*

Today, he values the input of not only his own associates but also a variety of other business contacts. He's learnt to ask people to be completely honest and he greatly values their feedback. He comments,

> *"We make mistakes in business. It is one of the risks of making decisions. But if you're prepared to learn from your mistakes and if you have good advisors, God will teach you through the experience. So even in the bad times, He's looking to teach you good lessons."*

Matt's Experience

Remember Matt, the self-employed painter and decorator, whose talents included playing team sports and being outdoors? As I continued my interview with Matt, he explained how after five years of ski and sun seasons he pursued a career climbing the corporate ladder. He joined a Travel company before moving to Sales in a large multinational company,

> *"First I drove about 70,000 miles a year, trekking round cash-and-carrys, hospitals, universities and other places who used all the products I was trying to sell. I was moved to a central role before switching companies and doing Category Management. After a few years I moved to a brewing company into Customer Marketing, working my way up to Customer Marketing Director in 2008.*
>
> *Hindsight is a wonderful thing, isn't it? It didn't feel right. I was struggling with it. It wasn't me. I was trying to be what this company wanted me to be, but didn't really know how to do it, because it just wasn't me. This culminated when I was kicked out, which at the time was really tough, but with hindsight was actually wonderful.*

I lost my job the same week Lehman Brothers went under, the start of the whole crash.[2] *Not a great time to be looking for a job, because companies had battened down the hatches and no one knew what was going on. I spent a few months looking for similar roles with no success. Whilst I was doing that, a friend from Church who was moving to a new house said, 'Oh, can you give us a hand just painting our kitchen?' So, I painted her kitchen for her. Then other people from Church started asking, 'If you've done that, could you just come and do this, whilst you've got a bit of time? We'll pay you obviously!' I wasn't sure how I felt about it, but agreed, "Okay, well, you can pay me a bit if you like." Then it just snowballed and I haven't stopped.*

After a few months, I decided, 'I'm so happy doing this and not being in the corporate world, let's do the sums and see if I can make this work.'

So, I took the plunge, registered as self-employed in 2009 and I haven't looked back since."

Now, it's time to think about your own career journey.

Start by considering the big picture. What does your career journey look like? Is it an upward curve? Does it have a downward trajectory? Is it hilly or mountainous with highs and lows? Most people have some ups and downs during their working lives. What were the causes of highs, lows and stable times? What skills have you picked up along the way? How did you make decisions about turning points? What life events impacted your career? You might need to make a list of your thoughts before you plot them on your own timeline.

If your career is short, focus on your childhood experiences. If it's longer, then focus on the major changes, the experiences which had the most impact for you. You may need to include personal circumstances on your timeline because events which happen in your personal life can have a significant impact on your career and working life. This is all part of life's rich tapestry, whether good or bad.

Next, mark on your timeline times when you felt close to Jesus, times when He felt further away and why was this? What was it about those times that made you feel close to or far away from God and how did you know? Where was Jesus in the stressful times? Where was He in your successful times? Make a note of any themes you notice. I find it fascinating to see where Jesus is making an impact in our careers; how is He working in your life as He was in Joseph's? Can you identify any golden threads?

Activity 18:
Your Career Journey

Take a large sheet of paper (or word document or excel spreadsheet).

Divide it in half horizontally by drawing a line across the middle of the paper from one side to the other.

Write your current age at the right-hand end of the line, and mark off relevant intervals going backwards in time until your birth at the left-hand end of the line.

The picture you draw of your career journey will include highs and lows joined together going across the page.

Note any significant positive experiences above the line, placing them higher up the page the more positive they are.

Note any significant negative experiences below the line, again marking them lower down the page the more negative they were.

You might find you need to write a list of all these events before committing them to your timeline.

Connect each significant event, positive or negative, to represent your career journey.

Mark on your timeline, in a new colour – times when you felt close to Jesus, times when He felt further away.

- What was it about those times which made you feel close or far away from God? How did you know?

Talk this through with someone you trust.

Make a separate note of any themes you notice, the major turning points, how you coped with negative experiences, any lessons learned, and anything you feel God is saying to you about your career journey.

Prayer

Father God, as I draw my career journey,
remind me of significant experiences that are
preparing me for what comes next.

In Jesus name, Amen.

YOUR ACHIEVEMENTS

'My son do not forget my teaching, but let your heart keep My commandments, for length of days and years of life and peace they will add to you. Let not steadfast love and faithfulness forsake you; bind them around your neck; write them on the tablet of your heart. So, you will find favour and good success in the sight of God and man'.

(Proverbs 3:1-4 ESV)

We live in a society which values achievement; our CVs include details of our achievements and we are asked in job interviews about our successes and achievements. The definition of achievement is 'a thing done successfully with effort, skill, or courage'.[3] Your past achievements can give you clues about your skills and strengths for the future. They are great places to glean the gifts God has given you.

Your achievements are about both successes and battles overcome so it's helpful to think about them in two ways. Firstly, the achievements you have found most satisfying and secondly, the achievements when you've had to overcome difficulties and obstacles. It is often said, we learn more from adversity and mistakes than from the good times.

The Bible is full of battles waged and won through the direction of God. There are stories of lives saved, people fed, people healed, for the glory of God. All great achievements. In fact, another definition of achievement is a representation of a coat of arms with all the adjuncts to which a bearer of arms is entitled. The coat of arms displays the achievements of the bearer, indicating which battles have been won; skills and strengths gained; and also describes qualities of the bearer.

One of the most outstanding achievements in the Bible is the rebuilding of the walls of Jerusalem in just 52 days described in Nehemiah 6:15.

Nehemiah was a cupbearer for King Artaxerxes in c444BC based in Susa (modern day Iran). He was living in exile, with many of his compatriots when he heard a devastating report about the ruin of his homeland Judea and specifically the capital city, Jerusalem. This upset him deeply. After a few days of fasting and mourning, he prayed to God, confessing and remembering God's promise of restoration if the community turned back to God. He also prayed for favour with King Artaxerxes, who noticed Nehemiah's sadness and sought to find out the cause. The King authorised Nehemiah's return to Jerusalem to rebuild the walls and Nehemiah secured letters of safe-conduct as well as access to wood from the king's forest to enable the rebuilding (Nehemiah 1-2:10).

Nehemiah travelled to Jerusalem. He secretly surveyed the city walls at night before gathering the officials, nobles, priests and other people who would be rebuilding the walls to share his vision of restoration. He said, "You see the trouble we are in: Jerusalem lies in ruins, and its gates have been burned with fire. Come, let us rebuild the wall of Jerusalem, and we will no longer be in disgrace." I also told them about the gracious hand of my God on me and what the king had said to me. They replied, "Let us start rebuilding." So they began this good work' (Nehemiah 2:17-18).

Over the next 52 days, Nehemiah organised the people to rebuild the wall and gates, assigning different groups of people to each section (Nehemiah 3). His efforts were not without opposition, which greatly discouraged the people (Nehemiah 4 and 6). He sought to encourage them by praying and relying on God. He devised a strategy of half the people building the wall and the other half providing security against attackers and marauders, able to rally calls for help when needed. He said, "Wherever you hear the sound of the trumpet, join us there. Our God will fight for us!" (Nehemiah 4:20). It seems they also worked around the clock!

'So we continued the work with half the men holding spears, from the first light of dawn till the stars came out. At that time, I also said to the people, "Have every man and his helper stay inside Jerusalem at night, so that they can serve us as guards by night and as workers by day.' Neither I nor my brothers nor my men nor the guards with me took off our clothes; each had his weapon, even when he went for water' (Nehemiah 4:21-23).

When the work was finished, Nehemiah gives glory to God. He says, "When all our enemies heard about this, all the surrounding nations were afraid and lost their self-confidence, because they realised that this work had been done with the help of our God" (Nehemiah 6:16).

What a fantastic achievement! As I read his story in the Old Testament, the career coach within me is wondering how Nehemiah would have described this achievement in his career? Throughout the story, we read of his reliance on God, his trust in God and his ability to encourage other people to stand firm in their faith in God so the vision God gave him could be completed. It must have been a deeply satisfying achievement for him.

Describing Your Satisfying Achievements

The STAR story-telling method is a great way of capturing the key elements of satisfying achievements. You start by briefly describing the **Situation**, then move onto the **Task,** or the goal. Then you describe the **Actions** you took, before stating the **Results**. This way you can capture what happened and what you gained so you can easily explain this to other people.

Imagine Nehemiah completing this exercise!

Start by briefly describing the **Situation**.
Nehemiah: *I was deeply distressed by the situation of my fellow Judaeans in Jerusalem. The city walls were lying in ruins with the gates burnt down. I was so saddened by this that my employer, King Artaxerxes, noticed and tasked me with rebuilding the walls.*

Then make a note of the **Task**.
Nehemiah: *The task was to rebuild the walls of Jerusalem so the city would not be disgraced and would be protected by renewed fortifications.*

List the **Actions** taken.
Nehemiah: *Firstly, I surveyed the ruined walls, then I shared a vision to rebuild them at a town hall meeting. I organised work-teams to rebuild each section of the wall. I oversaw publicity and averted any negative PR so that my teams remained encouraged. I organised security and oversaw the work schedules of the people. I remained steadfast in my pursuit of my vision.*

What was the **Result**?
Nehemiah: *The wall was completed in 52 days, on time and on budget! The people were galvanised to work together and the walls of the city of Jerusalem were restored and God was glorified. I am so proud of the way the people came together and worked ceaselessly to complete this huge project, overcoming opposition and disbelief that it could be done. I find it deeply satisfying to see what people can accomplish when they put*

their trust in God.

This is a great story of Nehemiah's reliance on God and his successful achievement. As you can see, the STAR framework provides a straight forward template to describe what happened. Here is an example using one of my own STAR satisfying career achievement stories.

Situation

After completing my degree, I worked for a company organising training courses throughout the UK. I really enjoyed this job! It was a small organisation so there was plenty of hands-on experience. However, there were no real opportunities for advancement, and I knew I would need to find another company to further my career. The tipping point was when I discovered that a male graduate colleague was being paid more than me for the same level job. This was the trigger for me to start job hunting.

Task

To find a new job with opportunities for career progression.

Actions

I started talking to contacts about what opportunities might be suitable for me. I knew I enjoyed organising and delivering training courses and wanted to do more of this. I was put in touch with an Independent HR Consultant who reviewed my CV, helped me redraft it, and pinpointed the type of 'training jobs' I could apply for. One of the jobs she identified was for a Training Assistant for Central Television. Little did she know of my dream to work in television! The job meant I would have to relocate, but I knew I met all the requirements on the job description and the person specification, so I wrote a covering letter to accompany my CV, outlining how I met the requirements of the job and why I was applying. I was shortlisted for interview and then the real work began! I researched all I could about the company and the job, even visiting the local Central TV news studio to pick up company brochures (this was before the days of Google).

I arrived early for the interview to get my bearings, and then answered the questions as best I could. And, yes, I had prepared some questions of my own. I was invited back for a second stage, which included meeting the HR Director, taking psychometric tests and a second interview with the Training Manager. Again, I prepared thoroughly. At this point I also spent time exploring the city where the job was located to see how it 'felt' as a place to relocate and live.

Result

I was offered the job. 250 people had applied so I was 'over the moon'! I was deeply satisfied because I had prepared thoroughly and performed well in the interviews and I knew there was opportunity for career development and progression (I later became Head of Training and Development). I felt my hard work researching and preparing had paid off. I had achieved my dream and I was so delighted to be joining the company.

I wasn't a practicing Christian at the time, but as I look back over my career journey, I can see how God was at work even then, meeting the desires of my heart and answering prayers I didn't know I was praying!

Maria's Achievement

Maria, the modern languages teacher we met in Chapter One: GIFTS, shared one of her significant achievements with me. First, let me bring you up to speed in her career journey.

Following her university degree Maria made a decision to gain a PGCE[4] teaching qualification. As a language student, she had often spent her summer months doing Teaching English as a Foreign Language (TEFL)[5] work and had found she got on well with young people and enjoyed the challenge of coming up with ideas to help them learn English. Becoming a teacher seemed an obvious next step. She spent the next few years as a Modern Languages teacher, then was promoted to Head of German, then Head of Languages, and Assistant Head. Following maternity leave, she took a sideways step teaching French and German in a job share. As her children grew, she went back to full-time teaching, became the Gifted and Talented Co-ordinator, and Newly Qualified Teacher (NQT) Mentor working towards being an Advanced Skills Teacher which meant she worked across several schools. She became Director of Languages and Assistant Head for teaching and learning.

Situation

"I was organising a trip to China, for students who were learning Chinese at our school to visit our sister school in Ningbo.

We didn't offer Chinese in our school and 2 years before this we hadn't had a sister school in China. I think this is how God works in the background, because I received an email, forwarded to me, from an organisation that was offering tutors in Beijing to provide free real-time online Chinese lessons, as part of an initiative to get people interested in learning Chinese. As Director of Languages, I discussed this with the Head who agreed I could offer these virtual lessons, if I could get a group of interested children together, which I did. So, each week, despite the nine-hour time difference, we met for an hour, which included 20 minutes of online tuition with the tutors in Beijing, followed by supplementary support and cultural learning which I provided. I didn't know any Chinese, so I had to learn really quickly and it was really interesting."

Task

"During this time, I got involved with the Confucius Institute[6] who were sending a teacher to China to set up a 'sister programme'[7] with Chinese Schools and the Head of our School asked me to go to China to represent our school. I went, signed the sister agreement and agreed to arrange a schools' exchange programme within the next 18 months, which at the time felt very daunting. The goals of the exchange were firstly, to build a relationship with our sister school in Ningbo; secondly, to put Chinese, as a language, in context; and thirdly to give our students a cultural insight through the experience of visiting China and the school and to build bonds between the students."

Actions

"As you can imagine the trip required a huge amount of planning and preparation. It took a year to plan. The students who had been studying Chinese with me were invited to apply for the exchange trip, were interviewed, and those successful raised the funds to travel. I can't

describe how complex the whole risk assessment was: China has very detailed documentation I needed to complete. It was very difficult, but we had all of it in place. We were flying from Heathrow to Paris, then Paris to Shanghai and on the day of departure when we got to Heathrow, one of the students collapsed as we were checking in. This is where I think God comes in! This student was still coherent but kept fainting. A paramedic was called to provide medical assistance and by the time we arrived at the departure gate the paramedic was not happy for the student to fly. So, as distressing as this was for the student, they were taken to hospital in England, where their parents were able to meet them, as the plane took off to Paris. If this student had been taken ill in Paris, we would not have been able to go forward. There were only two members of staff on the trip and we would have had to stay in Paris with the ill student, until their parents arrived, putting the whole exchange in jeopardy since we wouldn't have made the connecting flight. I can only imagine how difficult it would have been if the student had taken ill on the long flight from Paris to Shanghai, or even during our stay in China. I feel God had a hand in the timing of this, although it was quite a traumatic start to our trip.

We were in China for 10 days, and the highlight was definitely the time we spent at our sister school in Ningbo. They were very welcoming and put on a big show for us. There was a big document to sign on a great big, long table, it felt a bit like the United Nations. Our students were really moved by the presents the Chinese children brought them, and the way the Chinese children related to them. We went to an elaborate tea ceremony, attended a calligraphy lesson, ate in their canteen using chopsticks. All our students took part in a cultural dancing lesson using red flags. Watching them was a joyful experience and full of laughter, because they would never have done this in England. They really stepped out of their comfort zones and it was lovely to see them give everything a go.

The Chinese set a high bar for us when we were organising their return visit to our school. We couldn't match their facilities or cultural activities. Instead, we did some home tech, or should I say food nutrition, and made something uniquely British like scones. We took them to our Design & Technology workshop which they didn't have in China, and they made wood carvings and picture frames, which they found fascinating. Our canteen was totally different to theirs as was our food, so it was quite an experience for them. The wonderful thing was seeing the emotional way the students reunited with each other because they had truly bonded during our trip to China."

Results

"I've organised a lot of exchanges and this was by far the biggest because it took a year and a bit of planning and we were traveling so far. We definitely met our goals of gaining an in-depth cultural insight, putting the Chinese language into context and building a good relationship with our sister school in Ningbo. Three years on and Chinese is still being taught at the school (now to GCSE level) with English students enrolled, not just Chinese origin students.

The school had already achieved the British Council International School Award[8] intermediate level, and through my work with the Chinese lessons, arranging the exchange and my connections with the Confucius Institute the school was awarded the full Accreditation International School Award, which was a great achievement with Chinese becoming part of the curriculum.

For me personally, it was linguistically fascinating. I learned some Chinese with the students, which I found interesting and something I'd like to continue because it's so different to the European languages I know. Professionally, I am so proud the school were able to set this up, and the students who participated so willingly. We were featured on the local TV news because it was quite special what we were doing. It was English students who wanted to learn Chinese who signed up for the initial real-time language lessons delivered by the tutors in Beijing. It was a fabulous experience, I loved being immersed in another culture, seeing the students experience this first-hand, and noticing hidden depths of the Chinese people was really interesting. It's stirred up those itchy feet again, to explore different cultures and languages, all because I responded to an email forwarded on to me, as if directly from God."

This is a wonderful achievement and Maria should rightly be proud of all she achieved and I'm thankful for the way she credits God. I know how hard she worked setting up the Chinese lessons and organising the exchange programme using the gifts and talents God has instilled in her. It clearly was a deeply satisfying achievement.

The STAR framework is a great way to share career experiences with other people because it provides the context, the goals, the steps which were taken and most importantly the results that were achieved.

Now it's time to consider your own successful achievement stories.

Activity 19: Your STAR Achievements

List the achievements you are most proud of. Try to make sure you have at least 5.

Flesh out each achievement using the STAR story telling method.

Describe the **Situation.**

Provide the context. This should be a specific event, rather than a generalised description. Note down key details about the context.

Note the **Task**, or the goal.

This should be the specific goal you wanted to achieve, or the task that needed to be completed.

Describe the **Actions** you took.

List the specific steps you took to achieve your task. Describe them in as much detail as you can. You might need to review them to see if any are left off.

State the **Results**.

Again, be specific and explain what the outcome was and your role in this. Explain what you accomplished and use facts and figures where possible rather than generalisations. Make a note of why you were proud of this result and what you found satisfying about this achievement.

Overcoming Career Difficulties

We learn a lot from overcoming difficulties, obstacles and barriers which impede our career and career progression. God does not promise us an easy journey, but he does not abandon us. 'Blessed is the one who perseveres under trial because, having stood the test, that person will receive the crown of life that the Lord has promised to those who love him' (James1:12).

We all have to overcome difficulties in our lives, or go through experiences which don't go as we'd planned or like;

- You may have worked with difficult people or bosses,
- You may have been made redundant, or sacked,
- You may have missed out on promotion, or not got the job you desperately wanted.
- You could have stayed in a job you hated because you needed the money, or because it fitted with other areas of your life, such as caring for family members, or
- You felt there was nothing else you could do.

Often, our personal lives affect our working lives and, we don't realise the skills and qualities we've gained through persevering and overcoming these challenges.

Hanna's Achievements

I interviewed Hanna, a cancer nurse specialist, to explore what she had learned from the difficult times in her career. Hanna trained as a nurse in Finland before moving to work in London, despite really wanting to be a missionary. She had spent three months of her nurse training in Kenya doing a student exchange and says,

> *"The biggest missionary organisation in Finland wanted at least two years of work experience, so I thought going to London would be a good step towards this."*

Life events, including getting married, intervened and she ended up moving to the Midlands. By then she had some experience in haematology (blood disorders) and so she was offered a secondment job in oncology (cancer and tumours).

> *"The first year in the job was really difficult. I hated every minute of it. Not quite every minute but every other, maybe. It was a really difficult job, and I found the transition from haematology to oncology quite difficult. I was employed to work with an oncology nurse practitioner who was super knowledgeable but had 'burnout'. When she wasn't there, a lot of people around me expected me to be able to do what she did. It was just overwhelming. I was learning a new speciality and getting to know the patients, some of whom died. I found it really hard but decided I would push on with my Finnish guts[9]; and then they made the job permanent! I found an empty cloakroom in the oncology clinic, rang my husband and cried. But somehow, in that time, I fell in love with the speciality. I guess I built up some professional resilience and as my knowledge increased, I became more confident and the job became less emotionally taxing."*

Hanna spent the next ten years working with a small research team doing clinical trials for breast and gynaecology cancer research, and then prostate, bladder, kidney, and testicular cancers.

"The job was really good for my confidence. I worked with people who believed in me. I think this makes such a difference and really helped me flourish. I loved the job and I loved the nurturing environment. It was so encouraging seeing drugs being developed coming into the mainstream, helping thousands of cancer patients live longer lives. Somewhere through that journey, I felt God was confirming oncology was my calling. Working with cancer patients was my thing."

For the last couple of years in this role Hanna was promoted to Team Leader.

"I was keen to learn the managerial side of things alongside my clinical work. The team grew from nine to fifteen people and whilst it was rewarding, suddenly going from peer to manager was not easy. From there I took on a hospital trust wide research matron job which hadn't existed before. It was a huge change. My boss didn't want me to do clinical work, so I was trying to build a team without doing any nursing myself. I found myself being away from the nursing environment to being stuck in an office wearing a suit thinking, "What the heck am I doing? This is not what I came here to do". But I didn't have the confidence to say, "My job doesn't look anything like the job you employed me to do". It was a very difficult time. The working environment became very toxic. One minute I was told I was lucky to have the job and the next minute I was told they couldn't manage without me. The changing goal posts, roles and constant change made it very difficult to leave.

I realised I really missed the patient contact, but I felt trapped because I was the main breadwinner in the family. I felt I had climbed the career ladder to get to this position which made it difficult to walk away from. It felt like a failure professionally. I realised I measured success by wanting to have more money, more status and more power but actually success doesn't have to be that way. It can be about doing what sits right with you, what drives you. You should follow your heart and do what makes you tick, rather than follow the herd going down the path everybody thinks you want to go down. When I was in that pokey office, wearing my suit, I really didn't feel successful.

I made the difficult decision to go back to a clinical role. I had lost my professional confidence, so it wasn't easy, but with the support of my prayer partners and listening to a sermon at Church about what gets you out of bed in the morning, I realised I had lost my passion for my work and I needed to get back my passion. I was praying for a job to land when a friend advised me, 'If you want out of there, you need to manage it as a project, think within three months you will have updated your CV, started to look at advertisements and started to tell your contacts.' Things literally fell into place. I was having dinner with an old colleague who connected me with someone else who encouraged me to apply for a job as a chemotherapy nurse. This job really helped me regain my confidence, rebuild my clinical skills and refocus on oncology nursing. A year later, I was able to apply for a nurse specialist role in prostate cancer, which I love!

Along the way, I felt guilty about not working as a missionary, because I had felt so strongly God was calling me to do this. I worried about going against what God wanted me to do because I fell in love and got stuck in England. Perhaps I should have been in Africa looking after different groups of people. Every now and then I would look for any short-term opportunities to work in Africa, but then I realised I'm in the wrong speciality because cancer is not really a big thing in the third world because there are so many other diseases. I also felt God was saying 'it's okay, you are working within your calling, doing what you are doing now.' I have made my peace with it because I can see how God's been with me along my career path even though it doesn't look how I thought it would look. I do feel God has given me a calling for working with cancer patients. Since the first year when I felt like quitting every day, it's become my special gift. It's such a privilege to look after patients and their families at their lowest point, knowing in their difficult times I can make a difference every day."

I found Hanna's story humbling and inspiring. I asked her what she had learnt from her experience.

"I learned how important it is to work in a supportive environment and work for somebody who you can respect and trust. I realised I can't work for somebody I can't trust or respect because it goes against my values and what I believe in. If my personal integrity is compromised on a daily basis, I can't do it. I realised even if I left it's not because I haven't achieved things, it was because I was rescuing myself from a horrible situation.

I learned a lot about the hospital trust business, which has given me a really wide view about what is happening in other areas of the hospital. Even though I worked in a niche research and management area, I felt what really made me tick was the patient contact.

I learned that God has been with me all the way even when I felt He's not been there and when maybe I haven't followed what He had planned for me. It's as if He's saying, 'Look at what you're doing every day, the people you are helping. It's no less valuable than working in the third world and actually, when I think about it now, He has led me to a different country!"

Tell your difficult stories, too.

What difficulties have you overcome? What were the results? What did you learn? Often these are the stories where we learn the most about ourselves. It can be helpful to use the CARL Model of Reflection[10] to flesh out these achievements.

This model is very similar to the STAR approach, but it focusses more on what you have learned from the experience. It includes:

- **Context** - Briefly describe the context of what you had to overcome.
- **Actions** - List the actions you took noting specific details.
- **Results** - What was the outcome? What happened as a result of your actions?
- **Learning** - What have you learned from this achievement? What would you do differently in a similar situation? What did you learn about yourself?

Make a note of your challenges, battles and obstacles you have overcome. Tell these stories in as much detail as you can remember. Then consider the lessons you have learned about yourself which will help in your future career.

Activity 20: Your CARL Achievements

Start by making a list of things you have overcome.

Then use the CARL Reflection model to flesh them out, paying close attention to what you have learned about yourself.

Tell the story of what happened.

Explain the **Context**.

Write down all the details of the context you can remember. Be as specific as you can.

State the **Actions** you took.

Make a note of all the actions and steps you took in this situation. You might need to go back over them to list them in the right order.

Note the **Results** or the outcome.

Record the outcome. Explain the difference made as a result of your actions.

Describe what you have **Learned**.

List everything you have learned from this situation, that you would do differently if you had a chance to do it all again.

Now review your satisfying achievements and career difficulties to identify your key takeaways.

- Where was God in all these things?
- How did your faith impact what you did, your successes and your battles won?

Use the next activity to help build up your faith.

Activity 21: Your Achievements Reviewed

Reflect on your STAR and CARL Achievements to see where God was at work in each situation.

- Where was God in your examples?
- Did He feel close or far away?
- Did you hear His still small voice inspiring you?
- How was He making good out of the bad?
- How was He working on your character through what you have learned?
- Are there any themes or patterns you can see?

Prayer

Father God remind me of the satisfying achievements in my life which are relevant to my career journey. Show me where I have had to overcome and the lessons You want me to learn from these unique experiences.

In Jesus name, Amen.

YOUR FRUIT

'You did not choose me, but I chose you and appointed you so that you might go and bear fruit - fruit that will last—and so that whatever you ask in my name the Father will give you'.

(John 15:16)

The fruit you bear through your work and career is made up of three things:

- the good works God has planned for you,
- the development of your character, and
- your Christian witness to others, believers and non-believers.

The word 'fruit' (as well as related words including 'fruits' and fruitful) is found 66 times in the New Testament.[11] It includes what you do as well as how you do it, both in your actions and in your motives.

How to identify good fruit?

Firstly, consider the good works God has planned for you in advance. As Paul writes, 'For we are God's handiwork, created in Christ Jesus to do good works, which God prepared in advance for us to do' (Ephesians 2:10).

Review Joseph's career journey and the good fruit he bore in feeding the people of Egypt and saving his family from starvation. Look a bit deeper and you can see the fruit Joseph bore for Potiphar, his great success in taking care of the household (Genesis 39:3), as well as the responsibility the prison warden gave him (Genesis 39:22-23). This shows how the good works God planned for him in advance prepared him for ruling Egypt.

God also made you and He planned '*good works*' for you to do. This is your contribution to the world. However small or large, it has value for God.

Think about your current job and the jobs you've had.

- What are the outcomes?
- What are you providing?
- What are you selling?
- What is your product, your service?
- What do other people get from your work?

It could be you are a call centre operative so your good work will be satisfied customers. Or, you are a GP so your good works are correctly diagnosing and treating patients. Or, you are a decorator and your good works are freshly painted rooms. As an electrician or a plumber your good works are in installing new devices or fixing broken items.

Secondly, the fruit you bear as your character develops. This is the fruit of your impact on other lives and becoming more like Jesus. Paul describes this fruit, '... the fruit of the Spirit is love, joy, peace, patience, kindness, goodness, faithfulness, gentleness and self-control. Against such things there is no law' (Galatians 5:22-23).

Again, remember Joseph and his character development as he goes from self-absorbed teenager to devoted brother, forgiving his brothers for their treachery. All this whilst he was governing Egypt with wisdom and insight, reliant on the God who interprets dreams and grants him favour. The man tasked with preparing the country for famine has been moulded by God to bear the fruit of character development which makes him more like Jesus.

These are the motives behind the way you behave at work. How is the fruit of the Spirit displayed through the work you do? Were you patient with the angry customer on the end of the phone in your call centre? Did you display love and peace when you shared a difficult diagnosis with a patient at the GP's surgery? Did you experience joy, and display this joy, when you painted the demanding customer's bathroom? Did you exercise self-control when you had to go and fix the same problem you fixed for a customer last week because they had broken it again?

How you do your work is really important in God's eyes. He wants you to 'live a life worthy of the Lord and please Him in every way: bearing fruit in every good work, growing in the knowledge of God' (Colossians 1:10).

Another thought to bear in mind, fruit doesn't grow like Jack's magic bean![12] It's not planted one night and fully grown the following morning. It takes time. It doesn't grow all at once and sometimes you don't realise it's growing until you look back. This is why it's a good idea to look back through your career journey and see where you can identify the fruit from the experiences you have had. Were there times, when God was growing a particular fruit in your life?

Thirdly, there is the fruit of your Christian witness to non-believers, people who will see your fruit and want to know where it comes from. This is coupled with your witness to other Christian believers who will be encouraged by the fruit they see in your working life. Jesus says, 'This is to my Father's glory, that you bear much fruit, showing yourselves to be my disciples' (John 15:8).

As a Christian, you are to be recognised by your fruit. You can't bear fruit on your own! Jesus reminds us we have to be connected to Him in order to grow fruit. Remember He says, "I am the vine; you are the branches. If you remain in me and I in you, you will bear much fruit; apart from me you can do nothing" (John 15:5).

Although this fruit is characterised in three different areas, your good works, your character development and your witness as a believer, it doesn't always grow in three distinct areas! Growth in one area can impact growth in another area. It could be through the good works you are doing, God is expanding your character and using these works to witness to non-believers at the same time.

David's Fruit

David, who has been designing and building landscape gardens for more than 30 years, talked about his career, and I could see fruit in all three of these areas.

Firstly, his business is creating wonderful outdoor spaces where people can relax and feel good. These are the works God has planned for him.

Secondly, he displays fruit in the way he interacts with his customers. He told a story about a job that went, *"terribly terribly wrong"*.

> *"This woman spoke to me as I'd never been spoken to before and went absolutely crazy at me. Even then, I had to show her my faith and show her my love and compassion and not walk away. Most people told me they would have just walked off thinking, 'I'm not working for you, I'm not prepared to do this and be spoken to this way'. But I felt a really strong conviction not to do that. Instead, I thought 'I'm going to do this and I'm going to bless them more than they've ever known."*

I was in awe of David's humility and compassion to this woman and how the fruit of his character was displayed through this incident in such a Christlike way.

Thirdly, people know he is a Christian. There are Christian symbols on his van, and he is open about his faith with customers and suppliers. He recently gave out palm crosses and cream eggs to employees of his local builders' merchants. Word of this spread to his customers and he finds conversations start to flow. He describes this as,

> *"A natural expression of who I am with complete strangers. Working with people, designing their gardens, means the relationship quickly becomes personal. They know I'm a Christian so even in the smallest moments I have the privilege to share Christ with them. One of the things I've learned is that I'm part of a huge work of God bringing people to faith along with many other people. It's not just me telling them about Jesus. Deep down the call is for everybody. It's how we live, how we're called to live our faith out."*

Not only is David displaying fruit by witnessing to clients, he is also discipling other Christians through his example.

Now, consider your fruit.

- Which themes emerge when you review your fruit?
- Are there any overlaps?

With many people I talk to, it's the third type of fruit they find difficult to identify. It's not always easy to share your faith at work and in your career, but people will notice, by your behaviour, and those interested may ask you why. In 1 Peter 3:15 it says, 'But in your hearts revere Christ as Lord.

Always be prepared to give an answer to everyone who asks you to give the reason for the hope that you have. But do this with gentleness and respect'.

Understanding that God is growing fruit in your career helps you to see your career from God's perspective, especially when your career is challenging.

- Are you going through a time of trial?
- What fruit is God growing in you?
- When you are flourishing, what fruit are you displaying for others to see?

Activity 22: Identify Your Fruit

Your Good Works

Think about your current role.

- What are the contributions you make?
- What are your 'good works'?
- What are you providing, selling, doing?

Your job description, if you have one, should provide clues about your good works.

Make a note of them.

Your Character Development

Ask God to reveal how the fruit of the Spirit is displayed in your work.

- Think back over your day – how did you respond to challenging situations?
- Think back over your week – how is God developing your character through your work?

- Think back over your year – is there any fruitful change in your character you can identify?

Make a note of your answers.

Your Christian Witness

- How is God using you, at work, to witness to other people?
- Is there any way you feel God prompting you to reach out to non-Christians?

Make a note of your answers.

Reflection

- Can you see any connections or themes between these three types of fruit? Make a note of these.

Prayer

Father God, thank You for the good works
You have planned for me. Help me to stay close
to You as You develop the fruit of character
in me. Please build my confidence to
witness to non-believers.

In Jesus name, Amen.

YOUR BLESSINGS

'From the fullness of His grace we have all received one blessing after another'.

(John 1:16 NIV 1984)

Did you know that God longs to bless you? When you flourish at work, this is God's blessing to you. In Genesis 12:2-3 God promises to bless Abraham, and to bless all peoples through him. In fact, God blessed Adam and Eve in the Garden of Eden. 'God blessed them and said to them, "Be fruitful and increase in number; fill the earth and subdue it. Rule over the fish in the sea and the birds in the sky and over every living creature that moves on the ground" (Genesis 1:28).

Adam and Eve disobeyed God and they ate the fruit of the tree of knowledge of good and evil and were exiled from the Garden of Eden, banished from God's presence. This set the tone of the fallen human condition. But our God is a merciful God, full of compassion and graciousness. He chose to restore the blessing through Abraham and to all generations through him culminating in the work of Jesus on the cross, and we are now blessed in the heavenly realms through Jesus (Ephesians 1:3).

What does this blessing entail? What did the blessing look like in the Garden of Eden? When Adam and Eve walked in the garden in the cool of the evening with God, they had many blessings. They had spiritual, emotional, physical, psychological and material blessings, everything they needed to live a fully blessed life.

Roy Godwin, who wrote *The Way of Blessing*, suggests this is covered by the concept of "Shalom" which is usually used as a declaration of peace and is still used by the Jewish community today as a term to bless people. Shalom encompasses peace, harmony, wholeness, completeness, prosperity, welfare and tranquillity. This includes blessing our bodies (health, protection, strength), our labour, (work, reward, security) our emotional life (joy, peace, hope), our social life (love, marriage, family, friends, community) and also our spiritual life (salvation, faith, grace).[13]

These were all blessings Adam and Eve experienced in the Garden of Eden, which were restored to Abraham; and then to us as spiritual descendants of Abraham though Jesus Christ, 'So those who rely on faith are blessed along with Abraham, the man of faith' (Galatians 3:9).

Do you think you have been blessed?

Look back over your career journey and consider how God has blessed you in these areas. Have you been blessed with meaningful work, fulfilling rewards and security? Do you experience joy, peace and hope in your career? So often, it's easier to focus on areas of our lives where we feel we have not been blessed. But actually, God is at work blessing us regardless of the circumstances of our lives.

Think back to Joseph. His father, Jacob, adored him and singled him out for special blessing (Genesis 37:3). His brothers were not impressed and sold him into captivity, but God still blessed him! We read, 'From the time he put him in charge of his household and all that he owned; the Lord blessed the household of the Egyptian because of Joseph. The blessing of the Lord was on everything Potiphar had, both in the house and in the field' (Genesis 39:5).

However, Joseph was falsely accused of a crime he didn't

commit and ended up in prison. Again, God blessed him! 'The Lord was with him; he showed him kindness and granted him favour in the eyes of the prison warden. So, the warden put Joseph in charge of all those held in the prison, and he was made responsible for all that was done there' (Genesis 39:21-22).

He found favour with Pharaoh, released from prison and was able to provide for his family when they came to Egypt, in time of severe famine. Regardless of his circumstances, whether with his family, slavery, prison or the palace, Joseph was blessed by God.

Whatever your circumstances in life, you can experience God's blessings, and this is through your working life as much as anywhere else. Sometimes, it's easier to notice those blessings when you are flourishing at work, when things are going well, when you are using your skills and talents to the full, when there are great results, and you feel 'in the flow.'

Joseph would have been able to fully identify these when he was elevated to work for Pharaoh. Just look at what he named his children. 'Joseph named his firstborn Manasseh and said, "It is because God has made me forget all my trouble and all my father's household." The second son he named Ephraim and said, "It is because God has made me fruitful in the land of my suffering" (Genesis 41:51-52).

He might not have found it quite so easy to identify these blessings earlier on in his career, but looking back over his career you can see where those blessings are evident. Sometimes, you need to look back at what you've been through to understand God's blessings, and how he blessed you in times of adversity and difficulty.

Matt's Blessings

As you have read earlier, Matt had a complete career change and now runs a painter and decorator business.

I asked him what he loved about it,

> *"I love being my own boss and being in charge of my own time. I go out and I work for a day and I get paid for it. It's as simple as that and it sits very comfortably with me. Looking back, I remember thinking "I know there's a plan. I just wish I knew what it was!"*

During the time when Matt was made redundant, he and his family had become very involved in their local Church, and Matt soon found he was involved in helping with children and youth work. He and his wife took on organising the annual Christian Aid fundraising activities including a large quiz night with food and drink and a specialist raffle. He says, *"It played to my strengths of organising events."*

Matt joined the Parish Church Council (PCC)[14] and served for over ten years eventually becoming Deputy Church Warden. His talents honed as a child and then as an adult were put to great use in his local church. He says, *"Life was good, but I wished I knew the point of all this?"*

A few years later, there was an opportunity to be part of a group of people from their Church joining another Church to help it become re-established. Matt and his wife decided to join this group and Matt soon found himself involved helping out and joining the PCC and has recently been elected as Church Warden. He says,

> *"I was given the right skills and being put in the right place by God, without necessarily knowing it's happened. All the things I did at my previous Church,*

all the things I was involved in, prepared me for what I'm doing now and being able to take on the Church Warden role without being fazed, because it's all in the memory bank. Looking back, knowing there was a plan, but wishing I knew what it was, it started to become clear. All those skills, all the experience was God's way of preparing me to do this. And the job I do means I have time for the Church Warden role as well.

One of the things I love about painting and decorating is I literally rock up, do a day's work, and go home. I don't carry any stress around work and frequently I have time to pop into the Church to do something that needs doing, on my way home from a job or first thing in the morning. So, it's not just the skills, but the time to be able to contribute. Looking back, knowing God was behind all this just makes perfect sense."

What an amazing blessing! Not only has God blessed Matt through his redundancy, but also through the intervening years He has been giving Matt the skills and experience he now draws on as Church Warden. He has blessed him with a job that he loves, which includes being outdoors, as well as the time to help rebuild a Christian community.

Maria's Blessings

Maria, who shared her amazing Chinese school exchange achievement, also told me about the blessings she has experienced in her career. She says,

"One of the things I learned a long time ago and I try to explain to new teachers, is you might love your subject, you might know for you it lit up a light and gave you joy and satisfaction and inspired you to take it further.

But you will teach many young people for whom your subject does nothing. They won't enjoy it. They won't see its relevance; they can't see the point of it and they hate doing it. I discovered it was about developing the right sort of relationship. You try and build a good relationship with your students and then they will work for you even if they don't like your subject. Actually, for me, it's about helping each student grow and work out how to overcome obstacles, how to hopefully have a broader mindset. Hopefully at the end of their time with me, they might not get some dazzling grade, but they will say 'I found that really interesting' or 'I enjoyed that' or 'I'm willing to go and visit other countries and talk to other people' or 'I'm not going to expect everyone to speak English because now I actually understand how difficult it is to learn another language.'

I think I learned that lesson in the first five or six years of teaching, because sometimes I would be working with a class where there were so many other challenges. The students might struggle with reading or writing English and they can't see why they have to learn French or German, because they can't even write properly in English. So, I had to find another way of connecting with those young people to let them realise that my subject matters, to help them understand that I noticed them, I encouraged them, even though this didn't always work. But I think this is the secret! The secret to how I teach is building relationships and helping students to develop and grow. This is what God has helped me with, and I wouldn't have known this at the start of my career, it's come through reflection on my experiences."

You can see how this realisation has been a blessing to Maria, and her students. She is full of God's wisdom and grace, as she encourages young people to learn.

Look back over your career journey.

- What blessings can you spot?
- When were you doing work which aligned with your talents, skills and strengths?
- When were you flourishing, and what was the cause?
- When were you blessed with great colleagues?
- When were you able to bless other people?
- How did God bless you in times of adversity?

Knowing how God has blessed you sets you up for success and can change your attitude to your career. This reminds you that God has a good plan for your life, and by being blessed in your career you can be a blessing to others.

Activity 23: Your Career Blessings

Look for your blessings by reviewing your career journey.

Start with times when you were flourishing. Make a note of how God blessed you.

- Did God bless you with meaningful work which made use of your talents, skills and strengths?
- Did He bless you with great colleagues?

- Did He bless you with opportunities for growth and development?
- Did He bless you with a time of stability, peace and prosperity?

Then move on to times when you were languishing.

Make a note of how God blessed you in this time, remember the gift of hindsight!

- What did you learn through this time?
- How was God growing your character?
- What was He teaching you?
- How are you benefiting now from what you went through?

Think back over the last day, week and month.

- How is God blessing you now?

Work quickly to list all the ways God is blessing you in your work. Include spiritual, emotional, physical, psychological and material blessings.

Spend some time thanking God for all these blessings and settle them in your heart by knowing God loves to bless you.

Prayer

Father God, thank You so much for all the blessings You have poured out on me during my career. Help me to recognise them as I look back over my career journey.

In Jesus name, Amen.

YOUR VALUES

'Again, the kingdom of heaven is like a merchant looking for fine pearls. When he found one of great value, he went away and sold everything he had and bought it'.

(Matthew 13:45-46)

Imagine the scene – it's the middle of the night, it's dark and you're fast asleep only to be woken dramatically by the fire alarm. You jump out of bed, smell the smoke and race to escape, your heart pumping fast. In those 60 seconds it takes you to get yourself together what are the things you grab as you make your escape? Is it your wallet? Your phone? Your passport? Your children? Your pet? Your Bible? What do you treasure the most and wouldn't want to lose in a fire? These are the things you really value.

Values are personal and specific. They are the things you hold in the highest regard. Your values guide your decision making, priorities and actions. Your values are important in the way you live and work and interact with other people. There can be a huge source of tension when your values are not aligned with the prevailing values in your work setting. Things can feel wrong or out of place and this can become a source of dissatisfaction. Conversely, when your values are aligned with those in your work setting, this can be a source of flourishing and deep satisfaction in your work. What you treasure in your heart can give you clues about your values. Jesus says, "For where your treasure is, there your heart will be also" (Matthew 6:21).

It's vital to know which values are important to you; and it's also useful to know which values are not important for you. Often, you might have a vague idea of your values, but unless you've really spent some time understanding what they are, this lack of clarity can affect every aspect of your working life. Often, it's easier to identify the ones which don't speak to your heart, rather than those which do, because they will be jarring for you.

For example, imagine you are part of a really successful team delivering a quality product ahead of time and budget and you feel really satisfied, what values are being met? Do you thrive when you are a full member of a team? Do you value quality? How important is it to you to deliver on time and on budget?

How would you feel if this team had failed to deliver? Are there any values in other people in the team which don't resonate with you? Was the product of inferior quality? Had time and effort been wasted? How personally would you take this failure?

Or, to take another example, imagine you work for a social enterprise finding employment for unemployed people. You love helping people and derive great satisfaction from seeing them get back on their feet into gainful employment. Your values of 'improving society' 'helping vulnerable people' 'supporting others' and 'providing a quality service' are being fully met. Then, a new regime of targets is set up and there is less money to support each person, so you feel compromised in what you can offer. You feel a tension, as meeting targets becomes the primary driver for the organisation rather than helping people. You realise your values are no longer in line with your work.

Some of your values are constant, whereas others might change over time. When you start out in your career you might be driven by ambition to succeed and be prepared to work all hours. But then, external circumstances, such as having a family, could change or re-prioritise some of your values.

Autonomy is a key value of mine, so I prefer to be my own boss and be in control of how I manage my time. I also love variety, so doing the same thing every day would be frustrating for me. Working with other people and building relationships is also important for me. I have always wanted to work with people, which is why I started my career supporting people in learning and development. One thing I love about career coaching is being able to help and support people. Since each person is unique, I also have the variety I enjoy. I love to learn and grow and so it's important I have an opportunity for this in my work as well.

For another person, having stability and knowing the processes they need to follow might be important; without this they might feel a bit lost. Someone else might value being busy and always having something to do with their time.

How do you know what your values are?

Look back over your career journey, identifying the peak career experiences and times you were flourishing, when God was blessing you, as well as the low points in your career.

Then, consider what values were present which either made this event or time really satisfying for you, or conversely what values were missing or jarring which contributed to the low points.

Note down these values and identify any themes or consistencies. Reflect on the ones which feel true to your sense of self.

Dewi's Values

Dewi, whose career journey we looked at earlier, described the values important to him.

The first is **'empowering others'**. Looking back, he could pinpoint a boss who empowered him and recognised his strengths and trusted him to get on with things. Dewi really valued this. He contrasted this with another boss who was very controlling and negative which made it hard for anyone in his team to take the initiative as they were fearful about how the boss might respond. Empowering others is a key value in running his business. He says,

> *"My strength is winning work and training people, recognising their skills and empowering them to use these skills."*

Another of his values is **'feedback'** creating an open culture where feedback is welcomed and honoured,

> *"I continually ask for feedback from my associates and people I work with, asking, "What worked well, what could be improved, what could we do better?" This fosters a culture of trust where changes can be made if needed. No offense is taken when feedback is honestly sought and given. I have found this to be extremely productive. It means issues don't fester and positive changes happen because I'm open to listening to the views of others and implementing their suggestions for improvement."*

A third value is **'generosity'**. He says,

> *"Being generous is important to me. I actively encourage my associates to be generous with clients and contacts by getting to meetings first in order*

to buy the coffees or a meal. This generosity and kindness creates a culture where people feel valued and clients want Silverlock to write their tenders because clients know we'll go the extra mile."

There's a consistency to this generosity which has built up over time. His business has become known for it and this is endorsed by other people, those who work for him and those who know him.

I've had the pleasure of knowing Dewi through the weekly Kingdom Business Network he runs. I can testify to his generosity, his willingness to receive feedback and his valuing of empowering others. What I notice is the values he displays create a culture where people can thrive. They also demonstrate a sense of God's heart for people.

Now it's time to identify your own values.

Reviewing your values is not a quick activity! It takes time to reflect on what's important to you as well as the things on which you would struggle to compromise. Take your time with this activity, leave it and go back to it a few times to see what really resonates or what gives you a sense of peace.

There are several ways to identify your values, here are two alternatives.

Activity 24: Know Your Values

1. You could ...

Review your career journey, noting the times when you were flourishing.

- Which values were present and helped you to flourish?

Next consider your low points.

- Which values were missing or jarring which contributed to these low points?

Note down these values, identify any themes or consistencies, and underline the ones which feel particularly true to your sense of self.

2. Or another way to explore your values ...

Grab a stack of yellow stickies, set a timer for 10 minutes and write a different value on each stickie, without judging what you're writing.

Use the question

- "What's important to you?"

Keep going until your timer alarm sounds.

Then group your stickies into groups which feature similar ideas.

Think of one word which encapsulates the ideas for each group.

Describe what this word means to you in one sentence.

Finally, rate these value words.

- Which ones are really important to you?

To do this activity interactively you could identify your values with a friend or family member to keep the ideas flowing and the energy high.

A day or two later, revisit your value words. Note down an example of when this value is present or is not present in your work at the moment, which could indicate a need for a change.

- Then ask yourself how do I display this value?

For each one think of any example of when it is apparent in your career.

Whichever method you choose limit yourself to no more than six top values.

They need to be meaningful for you and you should be able to remember them!

Prayer

Father God, I ask Your Holy Spirit to reveal the values which are most important to me.

In Jesus name, Amen.

REFLECTION ACTIVITY: YOUR CAREER EXPERIENCE SHIELD

This chapter has covered the vast canopy of your life and career experience. Now, it's time to review your experiences and create a picture of the key themes, lessons learned, achievements, 'fruit', blessings and values which are relevant to your career.

Put everything together in one place so you can create your career experience shield.

Use brief words and pictures as items on your shield, so it encapsulates all the important elements of your career experience.

Consider these questions.

- What are the key experiences you have gained from your career journey?
- What are the lessons learned?
- What are your key achievements?
- What Godly 'fruit' are you displaying?
- How could you display more Godly 'fruit' in your career?
- What blessings God has given you in your career?
- What was your experience of God's grace when you were flourishing in your career?
- How did you experience blessings when you were not flourishing?
- What are your top values?

Draw the outline of a shield on a piece of paper and use your answers to write words or draw pictures on your shield which represent your career experiences.

I recommend you really get your creative juices flowing and use colour and drawings as far as possible.

Prayer

Father God, thank You so much for all the career experiences You have given me; for my achievements, and things I have overcome, the Godly fruit I display, and Your blessings. Thank You for the values You have given me, help me identify ones which are most important to You.

In Jesus name, Amen.

GRACE

Gifts
Relationships
Abilities
Curiosities
Experiences

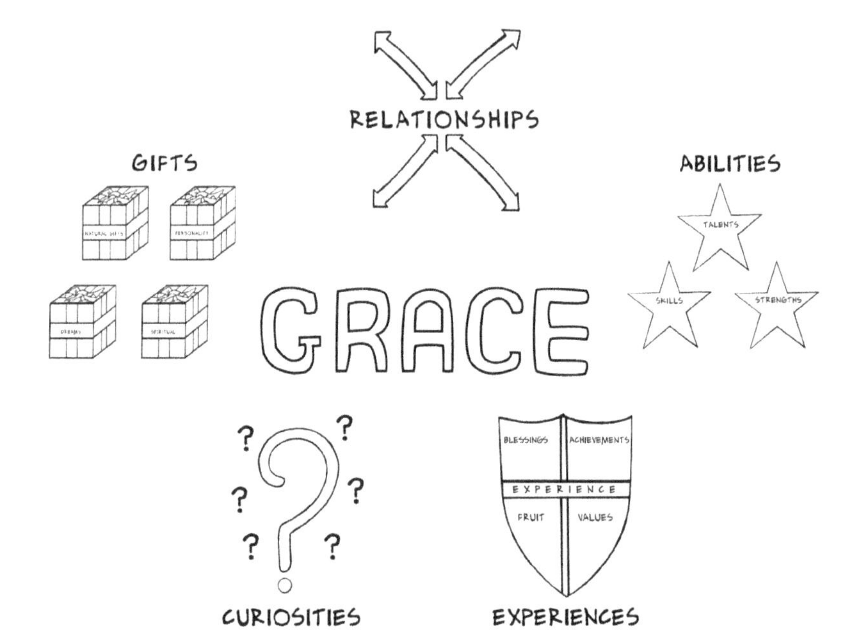
RELATIONSHIPS
GIFTS
NATURAL GIFTS
PERSONALITY
DREAMS
SPIRITUAL
ABILITIES
TALENTS
SKILLS
STRENGTHS
GRACE
BLESSINGS
ACHIEVEMENTS
EXPERIENCE
FRUIT
VALUES
CURIOSITIES
EXPERIENCES

Chapter Six: GOD'S GRACE FOR YOU

'For it is by grace you have been saved, through faith – and this is not from yourselves, it is the gift of God – not by works, so that no one can boast'.

(Ephesians 2:8-9)

God has given you all the **GRACE** you need for your career and as you have used this book to help you explore your Gifts, Relationships, Abilities, Curiosities and Experiences you will have seen the uniqueness in the way you are '*knit together*' (Psalm 139:13). Also, as I've shared some of my story with you, and stories of others via the interviews you will see each person's story is unique. However, they share one thing in common. They are all followers of Jesus Christ.

It has been fascinating to hear the difference this has made and to see how God has been and is at work in their careers and workplaces. God makes a difference in your career as well, as you can see how uniquely He made you, and how the **GRACE** He has given for your career can impact the choices you make for your future.

Jesus says to His followers, "You are the salt of the earth" (Matthew 5:13) and as Christians we are meant to bring a distinctive flavour to our work situations, similar to the way salt flavours food. We do this is by embracing the values of God's Kingdom in our workplaces. These are Godly values which people who are members of God's Kingdom display. I refer to them as Kingdom values.

These Kingdom values are often counter-cultural and when we demonstrate them in our working lives, they bring honour to God, and help us grow more like Jesus. Kingdom values take us beyond what we might think of as our own personal values which we explored in the last chapter. They demonstrate God's impact in your career and the distinctiveness being a follower of Jesus can make to your working life.

As I write this chapter, the country is mourning the late Queen Elizabeth II. Time and time again commentators have noted the way she carried out her duties and how this was based on her Christian faith, and the Christian values she held dear. People noticed this distinctiveness and she shone the light on Jesus as the source.

You could have completed your career exploration without any mention of Christian faith, but it is my view that God's perspective makes all the difference. When you understand He has made you uniquely for a purpose and you find the career path He prepared for you, you will find you can flourish at work.

Now, is the time to pull everything together, to consider what you have discovered about yourself. It's time to display God's **GRACE** for your career paying particular attention to God's perspective, His Kingdom values. From this you can draw up a blueprint for your career and then identify God's purpose for your career.

In this chapter, you will explore which **Kingdom Values** God has placed on your heart and how you might express them in your career. You will also review all the **GRACE Unwrapped** God has given you for your career and display it in one place. Finally, you will have the opportunity to draw up the **Career Blueprint** God has for your future using all the clues He has left along the way. Your Career Blueprint lays the foundation for God's purposes for your career and from it you will compose your **Career Purpose**.

Prayer

Father God, as I explore Your Kingdom values, and draw together all the strands of Your **GRACE** for my career, prompt me through Your Holy Spirit to construct a career blueprint which is authentic and exciting and points to Your purpose for my career.

In Jesus name, Amen.

KINGDOM VALUES

'Those who live according to the flesh have their minds set on what the flesh desires; but those who live in accordance with the Spirit have their minds set on what the Spirit desires'.

(Romans 8:5)

God's Kingdom values remind us of the spiritual element of our working lives and the difference following Jesus makes in our careers, but they are not always easy to adopt and display.

For example, I place a high value on 'Autonomy' in my career, but this doesn't always fit with God's requirement for me to be obedient to his leading. I may have to abandon my desire to do what I want, when I want, so I can follow Him and do what He wants when He wants. As you can imagine, this can present a challenge for me. Invariably, when I follow His way rather than go my own way, I have a sense of peace about the route I am taking. As I've submitted more and more to God's will and learned to value His values above my own, I've had more peace and experienced more joy about the direction He wants to take me in my career.

What are God's values?

- What are the things which are close to His heart?
- How might you reflect His values in the workplace and in your career so you point people to God?
- How might you align what God's values are for your career with what you want?
- How do you know if the career you want fits with God's values?

Obedience

Obedience is a deeply counter-cultural value. It's not a word you will find in a list of work-values, and yet God values obedience highly. It matters to Him when you are obedient, when you choose to trust Him in all things. Jesus, our supreme example, was obedient to God even to death on the cross (Philippians 2:8). Sometimes, this can be uncomfortable or painful for us, as it was for Jesus, but our obedience demonstrates our love for God above everything else. Jesus says, "If you love me, keep my commands" (John 14:15).

There are some careers where obedience matters, such as in the Armed Forces, so orders can be carried out unquestioningly, but for most people working in 'civvy street' this is much harder. We are used to a certain level of freedom to make choices about what we do, within the framework of our job description. We don't always have to follow specific commands, but we generally do have to meet certain expectations.

So, what does being obedient in your work and your career mean to you? Does it mean changing direction to do something different? Does it mean staying where you are? Does it mean doing what your boss wants, even though you might disagree?

This Kingdom value is about making a deliberate choice to be obedient to God's leading out of love for Him. He loves it when we choose His will above our own, but He leaves this choice to us.

Humility

Jesus humbled Himself by becoming obedient (Philippians 2:8 again) demonstrating the link between humility and obedience. This is a really interesting Kingdom value because it is not what you would expect to see in a dog-eat-dog world, where humility can be viewed as a negative rather than a positive. When I completed my first Strengths Profile© **'Humility'**, *'You are happy to stay in the background, giving others credit for your contributions,'* was my fifth ranked strength. Initially, I was surprised and a bit annoyed! I felt 'Humility' would get in the way of promoting myself; in fact, I found I used 'Humility' as an excuse not to promote myself as a career coach, allowing 'false pride' to get in the way.

What does humility mean to God? It's the opposite of pride in ourselves. This is not to say pride in our work isn't a valuable thing because it is. We can take pride in a job well done as long as we give the glory to God. Being humble is about putting other people first, especially God!

Forgiveness

Forgiving is not easy! It's easier to get caught up in our own hurt, pain, self-righteousness, anger and grief. Forgiveness is not an emotion, it is an act of will, a decision you take. Lack of forgiveness can really hold you back in your work and career, which seems strange when you are the one who has been wronged.

Do you find yourself 'stuck' in the past over a hurt or spending most of your time fretting over an issue which has caused you grief? Then, it's likely you need to forgive someone. Steve Goss writes in *Freedom in Christ* how forgiving from the heart helps you move on because it's 'for our own sake that we forgive. We think that by forgiving someone we let them off the hook – but by not forgiving them we stay hooked to the pain and the past'.[1]

As a Kingdom value how does forgiveness play out in your career? What does forgiving look like in your workplace? Do you seek out opportunities to forgive? Do you regularly forgive those who hurt you, colleagues, clients, customers, suppliers, your boss? By regularly forgiving the small things which wrong you, you can build up a habit which helps when you need to forgive big issues.

It also helps to remember how much God has forgiven you and what He does with your sins. 'Once again You will have compassion on us. You will trample our sins under Your feet and throw them into the depths of the ocean!' (Micah 7:19 NLT). They are gone forever.

Holiness

Holiness is a key Kingdom value. Holiness is the mark of being a Christian which really sets us apart. Peter reminds his readers, 'for it is written: 'Be holy, because I am holy' (1 Peter 1:16). God is inherently holy and he calls us to be holy, set apart for His purposes. Holiness is the absence of sin and the beautiful, glorious perfection of God. The bar is set really high, and we can only be made holy through Jesus' sacrifice on the cross (Hebrews 10:10). It's Jesus' holiness shining through us as we co-operate with the work of the Holy Spirit within us.

Nicky Gumbel hits the spot with his Bible in One Year notes; 'Holiness is not an optional extra. It is not just for saints and special Christians. It should be something we all aspire to in this life. Holiness is not the same thing as intensity. Intensity is not a fruit of the Holy Spirit! ... As C.S. Lewis wrote, 'How little people know who think that holiness is dull. When one meets the real thing... it is irresistible.'[2]

Again, it's unlikely you will find Holiness in a list of work-values! I find it intriguing that a Kingdom value, so different from what the world expects as a value, can make such a difference in a workplace or a career. It's not about being holier than thou, it's an active choice to let Jesus shine through you wherever you are.

God's love for us and our response to love Him and our neighbours underpins all Kingdom values. Jesus says, "Love the Lord your God with all your heart and with all your soul and with all your strength and with all your mind; and Love your neighbour as yourself" (Luke 10:27).

The *BizMin Course* (for Kingdom entrepreneurs) expounds the importance of The Great Commandment and looks at the centrality of love at work and how to love your neighbour, employees and customers, describing love as an 'attitude of the heart'.[3] This starts with the extravagance of God's love for us. Our response to His love is demonstrated in how we love other people.

At least two of the people I interviewed told me stories of how they found it difficult to love some of the people they work with. The response from both these people has been to make a decision to love the 'difficult person'. God's reaction to their decision has been to fill those relationships with love. This is not a forced love, it's a willing love which unifies and encourages. I know this works because I've tried it too! Do you struggle to love someone at work or in your career? Make a commitment to love them and let Jesus do the rest.

Kingdom values are driven by love for God and love for others. They are often counter-cultural, just as Jesus was counter-cultural. Displaying Kingdom values in the workplace can be challenging, but we have not been left to do this on our own.

The Holy Spirit leads and guides us in all things, as we make a decision, a choice, to co-operate with Him and display Kingdom values in our careers.

Identifying Your Kingdom Values

In this section, I have identified four Kingdom values, but there are many more I could have considered, Excellence, Faithfulness, Generosity, Hospitality, Honouring Others, Honesty, Justice, Kindness, Patience, Peace, Servanthood, Stewardship, Trustworthiness and Unity. It helps to consider how these Kingdom values are played out in a spiritual way, rather than a temporal way. This is what makes them Kingdom values!

As you discern the Kingdom values God wants you to focus on, it's important you use your own words and make sure you know what the Kingdom value means to you, as well as how it's evident in your work or career. As you ponder and pray about the Kingdom values God wants you to display in your career, make a note of them, and find a Bible verse or two to pin this value to God's Kingdom. Then describe what this Kingdom value means to you in practice.

You could argue all these Kingdom values are important, and I would agree! However, there is a time and season for everything (Ecclesiastes 3:1) and therefore I recommend you focus on the two or three which really tug at your heart strings.

Stewardship is a Kingdom value which resonates with me. The following is an example of the process to identify and describe your selection of Kingdom values and consider how they impact your career.

Stewardship

- 'Each of you should use whatever gift you have received to serve others, as faithful stewards of God's grace in its various forms' (1 Peter 4:10).
- 'Whatever you do, work at it with all your heart, as working for the Lord, not for human masters' (Colossians 3:23).

For me, this means making the most of the gifts God has given me to serve other people to the best of my ability. My aim is to help people as best I can through career coaching, focusing on working for Jesus, rather than myself.

Then, I consider how well I am doing at displaying this Kingdom value? How am I demonstrating stewardship at work and in my career? This can be a daily challenge, but when I remember to pray and to put God first my perspective shifts to a more spiritual place. I ask myself what are the overlaps with my personal values? What are the contradictions or the clashes? How might this Kingdom value become more prevalent in my career? What steps can I take to make this happen?

For me, this Kingdom value is about how I share what I have with my clients. For other people it could be about how they steward the earth and all the resources they have, it might mean how they look after God's creation, stewarding it for future generations.

Which Kingdom values do you display in your career?

Take some time now to pray and identify the Kingdom values most close to your heart.

- Which Kingdom values resonate with you?
- How are they displayed and acted out in your behaviour and actions?
- Are there any you feel which God might want you to develop further?

You could share your thoughts with one of your trusted friends. Remember we are all works in progress! Aligning yourself with God's Kingdom values and becoming more like Jesus is a process.

Activity 25: Identifying Your Kingdom Values

Spend some time in prayer and worship.

Consider which two or three Kingdom values resonate with you and your career.

Make a note of these and describe what they mean in your own words.

Find a verse or two in the Bible to pin this value to God's Kingdom. You will find a selection to get you started in Appendix Three.

Rate yourself on a scale of 1 - 10 where 10 indicates you display this value all the time, and 1 indicates you do not.

- How well I am demonstrating... (insert your Kingdom Value)?
- Rate yourself on a scale of 1-10 where 10 indicates you display this value all the time, and 1 indicates you do not.

  1, 2, 3, 4, 5, 6, 7, 8, 9, 10

- Consider, what are the overlaps with your personal values?
- What are the contradictions or the clashes?
- How might this Kingdom value become more prevalent in your career?
- What steps can you take to make this happen?

Prayer

Father God, thank You for the wonderful example set by Jesus in displaying Kingdom values. Help me to grow more and more like Jesus as I display Kingdom values in my career.

In Jesus name, Amen.

YOUR GRACE UNWRAPPED

'And God will generously provide all you need. Then you will always have everything you need and plenty left over to share with others'.

(2 Corinthians 9:8 NLT)

The whole point of this book is that God has given you everything you need for your career; the skills, the dreams, the experiences, your personality. When you figure out what all these things are, the way God put you together, you can identify the blueprint which makes you unique and then be more able to align your work with God's purpose in mind. When they are gathered together and displayed in one place where you can see them, you can then make decisions about what you want to do with them.

- Which skills does God want you to use more of?
- How have your experiences shaped you for what God wants you to do next?
- Which values are you going to use straight away?
- Which areas need time to grow and develop a bit?
- Which ideas need a bit more exploration for the future in terms of how you might use them?
- What have you learnt about the unique package of **GRACE** God has given you for your career?

Think about the presents you might have received as a child at Christmas; the box of Lego® which comes in lots of pieces and has to be carefully assembled following the instructions. Or, consider the paints you received which will only come alive as you start to use them on a blank canvas, or the new books which are crisp and ready for reading.

As an adult you might have received garden tools which are waiting for a clear day to be used in the garden; new clothes to be worn rather than just hung in a cupboard. Or, a box of chocolates ready to be eaten straight away! Amongst the torn wrapping paper and untied ribbon, there is a pile of items ready to be explored, used and enjoyed.

Think of this image, of unwrapping Christmas presents, as you gather together all the ideas and themes you have uncovered from the **GRACE** God has given you for your career. It's time to collect them all into one place.

Activity 26: Your GRACE Displayed

This might take some time, so make yourself a drink and settle down somewhere uninterrupted. You could put some background worship music on. This is your time with God to unwrap His **GRACE** for your career.

You may find it helps to display all this information in a visual way, so take a large sheet of paper and draw five large boxes, one each for the Gifts, Relationships, Abilities, Curiosities and Experiences you have uncovered.

Your aim is to summarise your findings, to begin the process of consolidation.

Review the Reflection Activities at the end of each chapter.

Fill each box with words, or images of the main findings from each area of your exploration.

Remember this is a summary, so condense your thoughts and ideas – be precise!

Your Gifts

- Of all the Gifts you identified which ones really stand out for you?
- Is it your natural gifts, or something about your personality, one of your dreams or is God prompting you to use your spiritual gifts?

Write down a few words or short phrases which crystalise your thoughts.

Your Relationships

- What have you learned about your relationship with God?
- Is He prompting you to spend more time with Him in prayer, in worship, or reading the Bible?
- What is He saying to you about your career?
- Who are your trusted friends and how might you nurture your relationships with these people?
- Who is in your wider network?
- How do you connect with them?
- Who are your role models?
- Which one is the most significant for you and why?
- What one lesson can you learn from them to apply in your life?

Make a note of your main thoughts.

Your Abilities

- What did you discover about your talents, skills and strengths?
- Which ones resonate with you the most?

- Which ones do you think God is asking you to use more?
- Which skills would you like to develop?
- Which unrealised strengths would you like to grow so you feel more energised and engaged in your career?

Note down key themes, using different coloured pens if this helps.

Your Curiosities

- What stood out for you as you explored your Vine of Curiosity?
- Are there topics in your education which are important, or is there knowledge you have gained which you would like to put to good use?
- How about the subjects which interest you; which ones would you like to pick up now and pursue?
- What things moved your heart to compassion and action?
- Do you sense God's prompting for you to do more in this area?
- What do you know in your inner wisdom? How do you feel about this? Is it time to act on this?
- What if anything, has God revealed to you?
- Which curiosities do you want to take forward?

Record anything which really stands out for you.

Your Experiences

- Which themes stand out for you from your career journey?
- What have you gained from your achievements and the difficulties you have overcome?
- What fruit have you seen?
- How has God blessed you?
- What are your key values, the things most important to you?
- How do they relate to God's Kingdom values?
- Are there any of these which particularly resonate for you as important for the next stage in your career?

Highlight areas which are really important to you.

At the end, why not draw a colourful outline for each box to remind yourself this **GRACE** is gift-wrapped by God, intended for good for your future.

Then display your **GRACE** unwrapped picture somewhere prominent and take some time to reflect on all you have learnt about yourself.

Prayer

Father God, thank You for the amazing unique **GRACE** You have given me for my career. Guide me with Your Holy Spirit as I consolidate all You have provided for my career in my personal **GRACE** filled package.

In Jesus name, Amen.

YOUR CAREER BLUEPRINT

'Remember, there is only one foundation, the one already laid: Jesus Christ'.

(1 Corinthians 3:11 MSG)

As a child, when I was at school, I remember learning about laying down good foundations. We were told the story about the man who built his house on solid rock contrasted with the man who built his house on the sand. When the storms of life came, the house built on a solid foundation stood firm, whilst the one on sand crashed and crumbled to the ground (Matthew 7:24-27). We drew a picture of a house on a rock alongside a pile of rubble on a beach. My imagination crafted a vision of a house on a rocky headland surrounded by raging sea crashing against the shoreline where the house on the beach lay in ruins. This vivid image remains with me, and I find it helpful to think of building a career on solid foundations. The solid foundation is Jesus and His blueprint for your career.

Traditionally, a blueprint is a photographic print made with white lines on a blue background showing how something will be made. It is the foundational document and plan from which the item, usually a house, will be built. Before a shovel is picked up or ground is broken, a blueprint is created. God has the blueprint for your career drawn up, and you will have discovered all the elements of it through the activities in this book. Your career blueprint provides the framework for your career from God's perspective, the way He created you to do the work He planned for you.

A blueprint is a drawing which provides the baseline for the finished product, it points to what the building is supposed to look like. When the house is built you can see it in all its facets, colours, and shapes. The blueprint pointed the way, but the building takes on a different dimension and characteristics as it is built. Blueprints can be revised, changed, and adjusted as time progresses, and this is the same for your career. With a solid career blueprint, based on what you know about yourself through Jesus, you can make effective career decisions, you can adapt to career changes and transitions whilst knowing and trusting God has designed you specifically for this.

The blueprint allows you to see all the pieces needed to plan for your career, from your personality, to what your key skills are, your interests, your values and your experiences. To draw up your own blueprint you need to revisit your **GRACE** displayed and ask some questions:

- What themes stand out?
- Which points seem to come up time and time again?
- What patterns or career clues can you identify?
- What is unique about you?
- Which items cause your heart to beat a bit more?
- How do your themes relate to God's Kingdom values?
- Which elements make you smile with delight and say 'Yes, this is me!'

It's time to take the items out of their **GRACE** boxes and explore how they work together in a way which is unique to you.

Your blueprint should include ....

- **Who you are?**

Which things from your **GRACE** displayed really connect with who God made you to be, the person He created in your mother's womb? This could include your personality, your natural gifts and talents, your values. From all the information you have gathered what makes you unique? Try to write a sentence or two describing who you are based on the **GRACE** you have unwrapped.

- **What you are good at?**

Include your talents, skills and strengths, and how you use them in a combination which is unique to you. Think about your achievements, what have you discovered you are good at from the challenges you have overcome, or successes achieved? Write down the most relevant or impactful to you.

- **What has God already done in your career?**

This could include dreams realised, prayers answered, blessings received. It will also include the people God has connected you with, the paths He has directed you down. Consider specific occasions or times in your career where you feel God might be preparing you for the future. What fruit have you seen in your career? How has He blessed you? How did your education or knowledge or interests set you up for your career so far?

- **What career clues has God given you?**

What significant dreams has God given you, in your childhood or more recently, which are as yet unrealised? What compassions make your heart beat faster so you feel compelled to act on them? Which interests intrigue you the most? What fruit do you think God might want you to grow or develop? Is there a spiritual gift you feel drawn to explore? What does your inner wisdom tell you? Has God given you any specific revelations? Which Kingdom value does God want you to develop in your career?

This is the process I used to write my own career blueprint, based on the **GRACE** God has given me. I noticed repetitions and patterns from across everything I had unpacked. It was really helpful to be able to draw from all the different areas to build up my career blueprint.

You will notice my career blueprint is a summary, it's not intended to be detailed.

Who am I? I love to read, to write, to plan, to help people. I am a sociable introvert (I need some reflective time on my own). I like to work with people, developing them or supporting them in some way. I value autonomy and variety and getting to know people. I am faith filled and love Jesus as the bedrock of my life, not just in my career.

What am I good at? I'm good at listening to people, coaching them and enabling them to develop and grow. I'm at my best when I'm on a mission, working towards results, and developing deep relationships.

What has God already done in my career? God has given me lots of experience of developing people and helping them grow. He's given me experience of interviewing people and using my insight to coach them. He's given me an interest in career development and expertise in how the job market works. He's blessed me with interesting and varied work, developing my skills as a learning and development specialist and then as a career coach. I've experienced how He has answered prayers throughout my career, building my relationship with Him as I learn to listen to Him each step of the way.

What career clues has God given me? I've always known I was meant to be a coach; I just wasn't sure what type of coach. The clue was in the fact that I was always fascinated by other people's careers and the choices they make (I'm releasing an inner 'Yes' as I write this!). My path often crossed with people who needed help with their CVs or discussions about their future careers. I long to help people who are stuck and don't know how to move forward in their career, to help them explore their career from God's perspective. I sense the spiritual gift God wants to grow in me is Intercession. It's exciting to be able to pray for clients and people I encounter in my working week. I also sense He wants to develop the Kingdom value of obedience in my career as I provide career coaching from a Christian perspective.

This career blueprint provides me with a framework to move forward in my career. The first two answers provide a summary of me as a person, and the second two focus on what's happened in the past and the clues I have gleaned about the direction I should go in. This gives me a foundation to make quality decisions about my future career.

It's time to create your own career blueprint.

As you pull all your themes and ideas together, see what they say about you. Consider what you have done in your career so far, and the clues God has given you for your future. Use this information to draw up your own career blueprint.

Activity 27:
Your Career Blueprint

Look at each area of your **GRACE** Displayed and highlight items which excite you or ideas which seem significant.

Write a sentence or two answering each of the following questions based on things highlighted in your **GRACE** Displayed.

Who are you?

- Which things from your **GRACE** Displayed really connect with who God made you to be, the person He created in your mother's womb?
- This could include your personality, your natural gifts and talents, your values.
- From all the information you have gathered what makes you unique?

Try to write a sentence or two describing who you are based on the **GRACE** you have unwrapped.

What are you good at?

- Include your talents, skills and strengths, and how you use them in a combination which is unique to you.
- Think about your achievements, what have you discovered you are good at from the challenges you have overcome, or successes achieved?
- Briefly note things down which seem relevant or impactful to you.

What has God already done in your career?

- This could include dreams realised, prayers answered, blessings received.
- It will also include the people God has connected you with, the paths He has directed you down.
- Consider specific occasions or times in your career where you feel God might be preparing you for the future.
- What fruit have you seen in your career?
- How has He blessed you?
- How did your education or knowledge or interests set you up for your career so far?

What career clues has God given you?

- What significant dreams has God given you, in your childhood or more recently, which are as yet unrealised?
- Which compassions make your heart beat a bit faster so that you feel you need to act on them?
- Which interests intrigue you the most?
- What fruit do you think God might want you to grow or develop?
- Is there a Spiritual gift you feel drawn to explore?
- What does your Inner Wisdom tell you?
- Has God given you any specific revelations?
- Which Kingdom value does God want you to develop in your career?

Remember, you are unique just as God made you so as you review what you have written ask yourself:

- Is this me?
- Is this authentic?

You should feel a sense of excitement or a sense of peace about how your blueprint uniquely fits you.

Take some time to thank God for this.

Prayer

Father God, thank You for the career blueprint You designed for me. Lead me by Your Holy Spirit to see the important themes and how they link together as I draw up my blueprint.

In Jesus name, Amen.

YOUR CAREER PURPOSE

'Many are the plans in a person's heart,
but it is the Lord's purpose that prevails'.
(Proverbs 19:21)

The great thing about your career blueprint is that it points to God's overall purpose for your career. So, when you've drawn up your blueprint, ask yourself,

- What does this tell me about God's purpose for my career?

Come up with a sentence or two. This career purpose is the bedrock for decisions and choices you make about your future career.

To give you an idea, here is my career purpose.

- To help people find their own career purpose and make positive decisions about their career which will lead to meaningful and satisfying work.

I'm sure this will not come as a surprise to you, having read this book! However, the point is, when you know your career purpose, you can make choices about your career based on this purpose. For example, I choose to work independently as a career coach, but I could work in an outplacement organisation helping people find their next job. I could work in an organisation doing career development (as I have in the past) or, I could work in education providing careers advice or guidance or careers support. There are many career support avenues I could pursue underpinned by my career purpose. I have the freedom to explore many different ways to fulfil this purpose.

Once you know your career purpose you can find work which helps you fulfil it, or you can work towards finding employment which fulfils it. The range of possibilities are vast and hopefully will fill you with excitement, as it does me. When your career purpose is aligned with God's purpose for your career, then the jobs you choose to do can be meaningful and satisfying, even as you travel along your career journey.

One of the joys for me as a career coach, is when people find career fulfilment, when they enjoy their work and know they are making a difference because the work they are doing is aligned with their career purpose. As a Christian, I am privileged to see God at work in people's careers and hear from people I have coached who are now doing something more closely aligned with their career purpose. When you know you are dearly loved by God, and He designed you with a purpose in mind, it is deeply satisfying when you find it.

I encourage you to write down your own career purpose.

Review you career blueprint and ask God, "What does all this tell me about Your purpose for my career?" Write down anything which comes to mind. The words you write should make you shout a resounding "YES!"

Activity 28: Your Career Purpose

Prayerfully invite the Holy Spirit to inspire you.

Review your career blueprint and ask yourself ...

- What does this tell me about God's purpose for my career?

Write down the words which come to mind, let this flow as a stream of consciousness.

Turn this into a sentence or two which describes your career purpose.

Notice how you feel about this.

- Are you excited?
- Do you have a sense of deep inner peace?
- Are you clear that this is God's purpose for you?

Let this settle for a day or two before returning to confirm it or make any changes you think God might be prompting you to add.

When you sense it's right for you put it somewhere you can see it, or memorise it, so that you have it hand when you need it.

Prayer

Father God, thank You that I am
uniquely designed and help me
identify my career purpose.

In Jesus name, Amen.

REFLECTION ACTIVITY: YOUR CAREER IN GOD'S HANDS

This final chapter focussed on career exploration from God's perspective. You've considered His Kingdom values and how they relate to your career. You've unwrapped the **GRACE** God has given you and displayed it somewhere prominent. You've identified important themes, drawn up your own career blueprint and penned your own career purpose.

Take time to thank God. Thank Him for His Kingdom values, and how He inspires you through His Holy Spirit

Thank Him for all the **GRACE** you have unwrapped for your career. Thank Him for how He has been and is at work in your career using all things for good.

Thank Him for your career blueprint which makes sense of all the **GRACE** He has given you.

And thank Him for your career purpose and ask Him to open doors for your work to be aligned with this.

Take time to thank God for leading you and holding you and your career in His loving hands, as it says in Psalm 139:10 'even there your hand will guide me, your right hand will hold me fast.'

Prayer

Father God, thank You for everything You have
given me, and everything You have done
in my career. Guide me as I take all I have
learned about myself and use it to take
the next steps in my career journey.
In Jesus name, Amen.

God doesn't just give us grace;
He gives us Jesus, the Lord of grace.

Joni Eareckson Tada

EPILOGUE

'But to each one of us grace has been given as Christ apportioned it'.
(Ephesians 4:7)

I began this book with the story of the Prodigal Son, and the father's amazing response of grace to both sons (Luke 15:11-32). It's a story about the lost being found, an olive branch being extended, of restoration and renewal. I love to let my mind wander and think about what happened next. The banquet has been joyful, the younger son is reinstated, the elder son is reunited (my hope) and plans are being made for the future.

The father looks on joyfully as his sons discuss their gifts and abilities. He smiles as they become embroiled in a conversation about their dreams and curiosities, the plans they have for the family business. He sighs with peace as they discuss their experiences, their achievements and the challenges they have overcome. The father knows the fruit they will go on to bear in their lives and careers, and he knows the blessings he longs to bestow on them as they co-labour with him. He knows they share Kingdom values. This parable is a metaphor of the love God has for each of us.

Both sons have choices to make about the **GRACE** they have been given. The offer is there, and it's there for you too. Unwrap the Father's **GRACE** and put it to good use, replete in the knowledge He made you for a specific purpose and He has good plans for you and your future career.

There may be times of transition in your career where you stop and consider what has gone before. There may be changes ahead, or decisions to be made. There may be times when you struggle in your career and there will be times when you flourish. I hope it will be helpful to return from time to time to God's **GRACE** for your career. Perhaps you will unwrap new gifts. Perhaps you will grow and develop your skills and strengths. Maybe you will explore new ideas and curiosities that will take you down new paths. Hopefully you will build strong relationships and grow closer to Jesus. And you will see how the experiences He walks you through are all part of the purpose He has for your career.

I'd like to close with some words from Apostle Paul, to encourage you to remember the **GRACE** God has given you for your career, to thank Him for all He has done in your career and all He will do. Praise Him for the **GIFTS** He has given you; the **RELATIONSHIPS** which enrich your life; the **ABILITIES** you make the most of; the **CURIOSITIES** which stir your mind and heart; the career **EXPERIENCES** which have shaped you as you look forward with hope to the journey to come.

'May the grace of the Lord Jesus Christ
and the love of God and the
fellowship of the Holy Spirit
be with you all'.

(2 Corinthians 13:14)

APPENDICES AND NOTES

Grace is the voice that calls us to change
and then gives us the power to pull it off.

Max Lucado

Appendix One: SPIRITUAL GIFTS SELF-ASSESSMENT CHECKLIST

Purpose

- To review your spiritual gifts and how you use them in your career or at work.

Introduction

Sometimes it's not obvious what your spiritual gifts are so this checklist has been designed to help you explore what you think your spiritual gifts might be. This checklist will give you an idea of what they are, but you won't really know unless you test them out! Spiritual gifts are used in the service of Christ to build up the Kingdom of God so as you complete this checklist think back on your own experience in serving Christ, in both your work and personal life.

Instructions

1. Pray for discernment from God as you review this checklist.

Prayer

Father God, You have given us spiritual gifts
to help build up the body of Christ,
reveal to me the gifts You have given me
as I work through this checklist.

In Jesus name, Amen.

2. Choose a wise and discerning Christian to go through it with you if possible.
3. For each spiritual gift think back on your own experience of serving Christ and consider if you think you have the gift. Your choices are 'yes', 'maybe' or 'no.'
4. Consider how you might be using this gift in your current workplace.
5. Complete the reflections at the end of the checklist.

The following tables are adapted from: Definitions Revd. Lee Proudlove; *Your SHAPE for God's Service*, by Amiel Mary E. Osmaston[1]; *S.H.A.P.E.* by Erik Rees.[2]

ADMINISTRATION			
A gift given to certain members of the body of Christ to enable others to work effectively together for the benefit of Christ's Kingdom.			
Luke 14:28-30; Acts 6:1-7; 1 Corinthians 12:28; Exodus 18:13-26			
If you have the gift of administration you are likely good at developing strategies, planning and goal setting. You might find you get involved in projects to make them more efficient and effective, or you could be managing or coordinating several different activities, and you thrive on organising people, tasks and events. You easily visualise what needs to be done.	**Yes**	**Maybe**	**No**
If Yes, how are you using this spiritual gift in your work to build up the body of Christ?			

APOSTLESHIP			
A gift given to certain members of the body of Christ to lay true foundations for a new work of God. (The original Greek meaning of the word is "sent one" – sent with authority or as an ambassador).			
Acts 15:22-35; 1 Corinthians 12:28; 2 Corinthians 12:12; Galatians 2:7-10; Ephesians 4:11-14; Romans 1:5; Acts 13:2-3			
If you have the gift of apostleship you may find you are drawn to opportunities to pioneer new things and have a keen sense of vision for the mission of God's Kingdom. You find you adapt easily to new situations and love to be an Ambassador for Christ. You may enjoy finding ways to share your faith in different cultures and environments and are keen to try new things for Christ.	**Yes**	**Maybe**	**No**
If Yes, how are you using this spiritual gift in your work to build up the body of Christ?			

CRAFTSMANSHIP			
A gift given to certain members of the body of Christ to plan, build, and work with their hands in construction environments to accomplish multiple ministry applications.			
Exodus 31:3-11; 35:31-35; Acts 9:36-39			
If you have the gift of craftsmanship you may find you are drawn to opportunities to work in a practical and artistic way with wood, materials, paints, metals or glass to create things that are useful or beautiful for the glory of God. You may find yourself mending things or designing things that will be of benefit to the Kingdom of God that will draw people closer to Him in worship, and you enjoy serving God creatively with your hands.	**Yes**	**Maybe**	**No**
If Yes, how are you using this spiritual gift in your work to build up the body of Christ?			

CREATIVE COMMUNICATION			
A gift given to certain members of the body of Christ to communicate creatively to share God's Word to believers and non-believers alike.			
Psalm 150; 2 Samuel 6:14-15; Mark 4:1-2, 33			
If you have the gift of creative communication, you may find you are drawn to opportunities to use the arts to communicate God's love and truth. This could be through music, drama, dance, writing, poetry, photography, graphics, art and you will love exploring how your artistry can help build up God's Kingdom through creative activities that glorify God and enrich worship.	**Yes**	**Maybe**	**No**
If Yes, how are you using this spiritual gift in your work to build up the body of Christ?			

DISCERNMENT A gift given to certain members of the body of Christ to discern the spiritual reality behind a certain situation or persons behaviour.			
Matthew 16:21-23; Acts 16:16-18; 1 Corinthians 12:10; 1 John 4:1-6			
If you have the gift of discernment, it's likely that you find you can tune into the spiritual environment to know when forces opposing God are active. You may also find you are given insight into the reasons for what seems to be happening, and that you can determine truth from falsehood. You will have clarity about whether something is from God or not and be able to test the spirits and look for fruit of the Holy Spirit.	**Yes**	**Maybe**	**No**
If Yes, how are you using this spiritual gift in your work to build up the body of Christ?			

ENCOURAGEMENT A gift given to certain members of the body of Christ to minister encouragement so other members of the body are strengthened and equipped.			
Romans 12:8; Hebrews 10:24-25; Acts 11:22-24; Acts15:30-32			
If you have the gift of encouragement you probably find you draw alongside people regularly to encourage them in life, and their walk with Jesus. You love to strengthen and reassure people who are discouraged, and to help them put their trust and hope in God. You often see the best in people and point out their gifts and strengths and how that impacts the body of Christ.	**Yes**	**Maybe**	**No**
If Yes, how are you using this spiritual gift in your work to build up the body of Christ?			

EVANGELISM			
A gift given to certain members of the body of Christ to effectively communicate the message of the gospel as a witness for Jesus Christ and to bring people into God's Kingdom.			
Acts 8:5-6; Acts 8:26-40; Acts 14:21; Luke 19:1-10			
If you have the gift of evangelism you may find you get excited about sharing your faith with non-believers and you seek opportunities to talk to people about spiritual matters. You have a sense when non-believers are receptive to Christ and long to bring more people into the Kingdom. You find you are drawn to evangelistic opportunities and have a heart for God's lost sheep.	**Yes**	**Maybe**	**No**
If Yes, how are you using this spiritual gift in your work to build up the body of Christ?			

FAITH			
A gift given to certain members of the body of Christ to discern with confidence the will and purposes of God for the future of His work.			
Acts 11:22-24; Romans 4:18-21; 1 Corinthians 12:9; 1 Corinthians13:2; Hebrews 11:1			
If you have the gift of faith you believe firmly in God and inspire others to trust Him. You may find yourself praying with passion and perseverance and expect God to answer your prayers, knowing that He will overcome all issues. You may be willing to take risks for your faith putting complete confidence in Jesus. You will be keen to step out in faith to see what God will do.	**Yes**	**Maybe**	**No**
If Yes, how are you using this spiritual gift in your work to build up the body of Christ?			

GIVING A gift given to certain members of the body of Christ to contribute their material resources to Christ's work with liberality and cheerfulness.			
Mark 12:41-44; Romans 12:8; 2 Corinthians 8:1-7; Luke 21:1-4			
If you have the gift of giving, you will find yourself giving time or money most cheerfully. You will be contributing and supporting Christian ventures that support and enable God's Kingdom to grow. You will be managing your finances and resources so that you can give away whatever God asks of you and you will long to support those less fortunate than yourself. You may also have a special ability to make money that can be used for God's purposes.	**Yes**	**Maybe**	**No**
If Yes, how are you using this spiritual gift in your work to build up the body of Christ?			

HEALING A gift given to certain members of the body of Christ to pray with confidence for the healing of others.			
Acts 3:1-10; Acts 9:32-41; Acts 28:7-10; 1 Corinthians 12:9, 28, 30; Mark 2:1-12			
If you have the gift of healing you may find you consistently pray for people and they are healed. You may be drawn to people who are suffering physically, mentally, emotionally or spiritually and know that God can heal them supernaturally. You may also find you care deeply for these people and long to see God heal them. You may also be able to bring comfort, relief and restoration to people who are suffering.	**Yes**	**Maybe**	**No**
If Yes, how are you using this spiritual gift in your work to build up the body of Christ?			

<table>
<tr><td colspan="4">HELPS
A gift given to certain members of the body of Christ to invest the talents they have in the life and ministry of others to help them achieve their God-given potential</td></tr>
<tr><td colspan="4">Mark 15:40-41; Acts 9:36; Romans 16:1-2; 1 Corinthians 12:28</td></tr>
<tr><td>If you have the gift of helps you may find you are drawn to people who are in need and long to help them. You may be able to spot needs easily and seek to help them from your own resources. You are drawn to people in difficult circumstances and feel a deep compassion for them and long to see them move into their God-given potential.</td><td>Yes</td><td>Maybe</td><td>No</td></tr>
<tr><td colspan="4">If Yes, how are you using this spiritual gift in your work to build up the body of Christ?</td></tr>
</table>

<table>
<tr><td colspan="4">HOSPITALITY
A gift given to certain members of the body of Christ to offer an open house and a warm welcome for the benefit of others.</td></tr>
<tr><td colspan="4">Acts 16:14-15; Romans 12:13; Romans 16:23; Hebrews 13:1-2; 1 Peter 4:9</td></tr>
<tr><td>If you have the gift of hospitality, you find it easy to welcome people and help them to feel at ease. You like to make people feel valued and cared for by meeting their needs for food, warmth, comfort and shelter. You are likely to really enjoy fellowship and seek out opportunities to provide comfortable spaces for this. You look out for people who are new and welcome them, and you draw in people who are shy or lonely so that they can feel a sense of belong to the body of Christ.</td><td>Yes</td><td>Maybe</td><td>No</td></tr>
<tr><td colspan="4">If Yes, how are you using this spiritual gift in your work to build up the body of Christ?</td></tr>
</table>

INTERCESSION			
A gift given to certain members of the body of Christ to stand in the gap in prayer for someone, something, or someplace, believing for profound results.			
Hebrews 7:25; Colossians 1:9-12, Colossians 4:12; James 5:14-16; Romans 8:26-27; John 17:9-26			
If you have the gift of intercession you will find yourself praying in all and any circumstances. You will make time to pray for other people and situations expecting God to hear your prayers and answer them. You may be very aware of the spiritual battle and see prayer as a weapon of love. You may respond to the Holy Spirit's prompting to pray and try to stay in God's will for a person, or situation.	**Yes**	**Maybe**	**No**
If Yes, how are you using this spiritual gift in your work to build up the body of Christ?			

INTERPRETATION OF TONGUES			
A gift given to certain members of the body of Christ to interpret a prayer or message spoken in Tongues.			
Acts 2:4-11; 1 Corinthians 12:10; 1 Corinthians 14:1-13; 1 Corinthians 14:26-28			
If you have the gift of interpretation of tongues you are willing to take the risk of sharing what you think God is saying through another person praying in tongues. You may be enabled to understand a language you have never learned and use this to build up people's faith. You may have clarity about what God is saying about a specific person or situation in a way that edifies, comforts and exhorts believers and glorifies God.	**Yes**	**Maybe**	**No**
If Yes, how are you using this spiritual gift in your work to build up the body of Christ?			

KNOWLEDGE A gift given to certain members of the body of Christ to gain spiritual understanding of a particular situation or circumstance.			
1 Corinthians 12:8; Colossians 2:2-5; Mark 2:8; John 1:45-50; John 4:16-19			
If you have the gift of knowledge, it's likely that you have insights or hunches about people and situations. You might be given specific knowledge or information from God that you could not have known naturally. You enjoy sharing your knowledge of the Bible and the Christian faith to enhance peoples' understanding of spiritual matters.	**Yes**	**Maybe**	**No**
If Yes, how are you using this spiritual gift in your work to build up the body of Christ?			

LEADERSHIP A gift given to certain members of the body of Christ to lead the church in its mission and ministry for the glory of God.			
Romans 12:8; Hebrews 13:17; Luke 22:25-26			
If you have the gift of leadership, you are likely to be drawn to leadership positions and enjoy inspiring people to follow you. You are able to share your vision of God's Kingdom with others and motivate and enable others to meet this vision in a way that you would not naturally envision, as if they are drawn by the Holy Spirit working through you. You may also be able to delegate to other people, providing opportunities for the vision to be accomplished for God's glory.	**Yes**	**Maybe**	**No**
If Yes, how are you using this spiritual gift in your work to build up the body of Christ?			

MERCY A gift given to certain members of the body of Christ to feel compassion for others and to translate that into cheerfully done deeds that reflect Christ's love.			
Matthew 9:35-36; Mark 9:41; Romans 12:8; Matthew 5:7; Mark 10:46-52; Luke 10:25-37			
If you have the gift of mercy you may find you notice other people's pain, grief and suffering and long to do something about it. You long to show people God's love and forgiveness through your own words and actions and will devote time to praying for and with people. You may find you are drawn to working in difficult circumstances, or in places where people are in need. You may also focus your time on issues of social justice and work to help restore dignity and wholeness to the glory of God.	**Yes**	**Maybe**	**No**
If Yes, how are you using this spiritual gift in your work to build up the body of Christ?			

MIRACLES A gift given to certain members of the body of Christ to pray with confidence for God to perform mighty acts establishing His Kingdom.			
Acts 9:36-42; Acts 19:11-12; Acts 20:7-12; 1 Corinthians 12:10, 28-29; John 2:1-11			
If you have the gift of miracles, you may be inspired by the Holy Spirit to pray for supernatural solutions to impossible situations and love to see God move in this way. You love how your faith and other's faith expands in response to miracles and love to see God display his power, so that people respond in awe and wonder.	**Yes**	**Maybe**	**No**
If Yes, how are you using this spiritual gift in your work to build up the body of Christ?			

<table>
<tr><td colspan="4">PASTOR/SHEPHERD
A gift given to certain members of the body of Christ to care for the emotional, physical and spiritual wellbeing of others.</td></tr>
<tr><td colspan="4">John 10:1-18; Ephesians 4:11-13; 1 Peter 5:1-4</td></tr>
<tr><td>If you have the gift of pastoring or shepherding, you may find yourself being concerned for the full wellbeing of people and spend your time providing guidance and helping them grow in faith. You thrive in building loving relationships and find that people confide in you and turn to you for support. You will have a deep sense of responsibility for the people God has put in your care and seek to know them personally and individually making them feel special and loved.</td><td>Yes</td><td>Maybe</td><td>No</td></tr>
<tr><td colspan="4">If Yes, how are you using this spiritual gift in your work to build up the body of Christ?</td></tr>
</table>

<table>
<tr><td colspan="4">PROPHECY
A gift given to certain members of the body of Christ to communicate God's truth calling people to a right relationship with God and/or to speak God's word in current/future situations.</td></tr>
<tr><td colspan="4">1 Corinthians 12:10, 28; 1 Corinthians 13:2; 1 Corinthians 14:1-4; Romans 12:6; 2 Peter 1:19-21</td></tr>
<tr><td>If you have the gift of prophecy, it's probable that you will feel a compulsion to tell people a message from God. You may find that God gives you words and messages for specific people or situations, which may expose sin, lead people to repentance and forgiveness or reveal God's character and heart. You may see truths before other people and feel called to challenge them to respond. You may feel a 'certainty' about God's plan for a specific situation or person.</td><td>Yes</td><td>Maybe</td><td>No</td></tr>
<tr><td colspan="4">If Yes, how are you using this spiritual gift in your work to build up the body of Christ?</td></tr>
</table>

<table>
<tr><td colspan="4">SERVICE
A gift given to certain members of the body of Christ to discern opportunities for service to Christ and a willingness to minister in whatever way is needed.</td></tr>
<tr><td colspan="4">Acts 6:1-7; Romans 12:7; Galatians 6:10; Titus 3:14</td></tr>
<tr><td>If you have the gift of service it's likely you will find yourself helping behind the scenes in a practical way, and that your worship of God is expressed through service to other people in the body of Christ. You may be good at spotting what needs to be done practically and find you are drawn to situations where you can be active in your support and that this is a loving service.</td><td>Yes</td><td>Maybe</td><td>No</td></tr>
<tr><td colspan="4">If Yes, how are you using this spiritual gift in your work to build up the body of Christ?</td></tr>
</table>

<table>
<tr><td colspan="4">TEACHING
A gift given to certain members of the body of Christ to communicate Biblical truth in such a way that others grow in their knowledge of Christ.</td></tr>
<tr><td colspan="4">Acts 18:24-28; Acts 20:20-21; 1 Corinthians 12:28-29; Ephesians 4:11-13; Romans 12:7</td></tr>
<tr><td>If you have the gift of teaching you likely love to share with other people what you are learning from God's Word. You may have a knack for explaining your insights in a way that is meaningful for other people and helps them grow in their knowledge of the Bible. You are able to communicate effectively, asking thoughtful questions and encouraging people to think and grow in confidence in their faith.</td><td>Yes</td><td>Maybe</td><td>No</td></tr>
<tr><td colspan="4">If Yes, how are you using this spiritual gift in your work to build up the body of Christ?</td></tr>
</table>

TONGUES (SPEAKING IN TONGUES)

A gift given to certain members of the body of Christ to pray and praise God in an unknown language or to communicate a message from God in the same way.

Acts 2:1-13; 1 Corinthians 12:10, 28-30; 1 Corinthians 13:1; 1 Corinthians 14:1-18

	Yes	Maybe	No
If you have the gift of speaking in tongues, you are enabled to pray in a spiritual language you have never learned. You find you use this language to worship God privately when human words are not enough to help you draw closer to God. You may feel prompted by the Holy Spirit to pray in tongues for other people to comfort and exhort them. If you pray in tongues in public worship, it's likely that there will be someone who can interpret tongues to translate.			

If Yes, how are you using this spiritual gift in your work to build up the body of Christ?

WISDOM (WORDS OF WISDOM)

A gift given to certain members of the body of Christ to know the mind of the Holy Spirit and speak wisdom into a given situation.

Acts 6:3,10; 1 Corinthians 2:6-16; 2 Corinthians 12:8; James 3:17; Ephesians 1:8

	Yes	Maybe	No
If you have the gift of words of wisdom you may find God inspires you with his wisdom for certain situations to build up the body of Christ. You may find that the Holy Spirit shows you God's will for a particular situation or person. You may find that people seek you out for advice and guidance based on your understanding of God's Word and your spiritual listening ears.			

If Yes, how are you using this spiritual gift in your work to build up the body of Christ?

Make a note of your main Spiritual Gifts

My Main Spiritual Gifts	How I Use This Gift at Work

Read the Bible passages given in the sections above which relate to each of your four main gifts. Ask God to speak to you through these, and spend some time listening to Him.

If you're not sure if God seems to be using these gifts through you in your work, then I encourage you to pray through them with a mature Christian who can help you discern how God is using you.

A state of mind that sees God
in everything is evidence of growth
in grace and a thankful heart.

Charles Finney

Appendix Two: STRENGTH DEFINITIONS FROM CAPPFINITY: STRENGTHS PROFILE©

Strengths Definitions

Action Motivating
You feel compelled to act immediately and decisively, being keen to learn as you go.

Adaptable Thinking
You juggle things to meet changing demands and find the best fit for your needs.

Adherence Thinking
You love to follow processes, operating firmly within rules and guidelines.

Adventure Motivating
You love to take risks and stretch yourself outside your comfort zone.

Authenticity Being
You are always true to yourself, even in the face of pressure from others.

Bounceback Motivating
You use setbacks as springboards to go on and achieve even more.

Catalyst Motivating
You love to motivate and inspire others to make things happen.

Centred Being
You have an inner composure and self-assurance, whatever the situation.

Change Agent Motivating
You are constantly involved with change, advocating for change and making it happen.

Compassion Relating
You really care about others, doing all you can to help and sympathise.

Competitive Motivating
You are constantly competing to win, wanting to perform better and be the best.

Connector Relating
You make connections between people, instinctively making links and introductions.

Counterpoint Communicating
You always bring a different viewpoint to others, whatever the situation or context.

Courage Being
You overcome your fears and do what you want to do in spite of them.

Creativity Thinking
You strive to produce work that is original, by creating and combining things in imaginative ways.

Curiosity Being
You are interested in everything, constantly seeking out new information and learning more.

Detail Thinking
You naturally focus on the small things that others easily miss, ensuring accuracy.

Drive Motivating
You are very self-motivated, pushing yourself hard to achieve what you want out of life.

Emotional Awareness Relating
You are acutely aware of the emotions and feelings of others.

Empathic Relating
You feel connected to others through your ability to understand what they are feeling.

Enabler Relating
You create the conditions for people to grow and develop for themselves.

Equality Relating
You ensure that everyone is treated equally, paying close attention to issues of fairness.

Esteem Builder Relating
You help others to believe in themselves and see what they are capable of achieving.

Explainer Communicating
You are able to simplify things so that others can understand.

Feedback Communicating
You provide fair and accurate feedback to others, to help them develop.

Gratitude Being
You are constantly thankful for the positive things in your life.

Growth Motivating
You are always looking for ways to grow and develop, whatever you are doing.

Humility Being
You are happy to stay in the background, giving others credit for your contributions.

Humour Communicating
You see the funny side of almost everything that happens - and make a joke of it.

Improver Motivating
You constantly look for better ways of doing things and how things can be improved.

Strengths Definitions

Incubator Thinking
You love to think deeply about things, to arrive at the best conclusion.

Innovation Thinking
You approach things in ingenious ways, coming up with new and different approaches.

Judgement Thinking
You enjoy making decisions and are able to make the right decision quickly and easily.

Legacy Being
You want to create things that will outlast you, delivering a positive and sustainable impact.

Listener Communicating
You are able to listen intently to and focus on what people say.

Mission Being
You pursue things that give you a sense of meaning and purpose in your life.

Moral Compass Being
You have a strong ethical code, always acting in accordance with what you believe is right.

Narrator Communicating
You love to tell stories and see the power of these stories to convey insights.

Optimism Thinking
You always maintain a positive attitude and outlook on life.

Organiser Thinking
You are exceptionally well-organised in everything you do.

Persistence Motivating
You achieve success by keeping going, particularly when things are difficult.

Personal Responsibility Being
You take ownership of your decisions and hold yourself accountable for your promises.

Personalisation Relating
You recognise everyone as a unique individual, noticing their subtle differences.

Persuasion Relating
You enjoy bringing others round to your way of thinking and winning their agreement.

Planner Thinking
You make plans for everything you do, covering all eventualities.

Prevention Thinking
You think ahead, to anticipate and prevent problems before they happen.

Pride Being
You strive to produce work that is of the highest standard and quality.

Rapport Builder Relating
You establish rapport and relationships with others quickly and easily.

Relationship Deepener Relating
You have a natural ability to form deep, long-lasting relationships with people.

Resilience Motivating
You take hardships in your stride, recovering quickly and getting on with things again.

Resolver Thinking
You love to solve problems, the more difficult the better.

Self-awareness Being
You know yourself well, understanding your own emotions and behaviour.

Self-belief Motivating
You are confident in your own abilities, knowing that you can achieve your goals.

Service Being
You are constantly looking for ways to help and serve others.

Spotlight Communicating
You love to be the focus of everyone's attention.

Strategic Awareness Thinking
You pay attention to the wider context and bigger picture to inform your decisions.

Time Optimiser Thinking
You maximise your time, to get the most out of whatever time you have available.

Unconditionality Being
You accept people for who and what they are, without ever judging them.

Work Ethic Motivating
You are very hard working, putting a lot of effort into everything you do.

Writer Communicating
You love to write, conveying your thoughts and ideas through the written word.

Appendix Three: BIBLE VERSES FOR KINGDOM VALUES

Here are a selection of verses you can use to pin to your Kingdom values.

Excellence

- 'But you are a chosen people, a royal priesthood, a holy nation, God's special possession, that you may declare the praises of Him who called you out of darkness into His wonderful light' (1 Peter 2:9).
- 'Then this Daniel became distinguished above all the other high officials and satraps, because an excellent spirit was in him. And the king planned to set him over the whole kingdom' (Daniel 6:3 ESV).
- 'Finally, brothers, whatever is true, whatever is honourable, whatever is just, whatever is pure, whatever is lovely, whatever is commendable, if there is any excellence, if there is anything worthy of praise, think about these things' (Philippians 4:8 ESV).
- 'But as you excel in everything—in faith, in speech, in knowledge, in all earnestness, and in our love for you—see that you excel in this act of grace also' (2 Corinthians 8:7 ESV).

Faithfulness

- 'Let love and faithfulness never leave you; bind them round your neck, write them on the tablet of your heart' (Proverbs 3:3).

- 'See, the enemy is puffed up; his desires are not upright—but the righteous person will live by his faithfulness' (Habakkuk 2:4).
- 'For Jesus was faithful to God who appointed Him High Priest, just as Moses also faithfully served in God's house' (Hebrews 3:2 TLB).
- 'His master replied, "Well done, good and faithful servant! You have been faithful with a few things; I will put you in charge of many things. Come and share your master's happiness!"' (Matthew 25:21).

Forgiveness

- '"For if you forgive men when they sin against you, your heavenly Father will also forgive you, but if you do not forgive men their sins, your Father will not forgive your sins" (Matthew 6:14-15).
- "Then Peter came to Jesus and asked, "Lord, how many times shall I forgive my brother or sister who sins against me? Up to seven times?" Jesus answered, "I tell you, not seven times, but seventy times seven" (Matthew 18:21-22).
- "As far as the east is from the west, so far has He removed our transgressions from us" (Psalm 103:12).
- 'Bear with each other and forgive one another if any of you has a grievance against someone. Forgive as the Lord forgave you' (Colossians 3:13).

Generosity

- "If anyone forces you to go one mile, go with them two miles. Give to the one who asks you, and do not turn away from the one who wants to borrow from you" (Matthew 5:41-42).

- "Sell your possessions and give to the poor. Provide purses for yourselves that will not wear out, a treasure in heaven that will never fail, where no thief comes near and no moth destroys" (Luke 12:33).
- 'But Zacchaeus stood up and said to the Lord, "Look, Lord! Here and now I give half of my possessions to the poor, and if I have cheated anybody out of anything, I will pay back four times the amount" (Luke 19:8).
- "Remember this: Whoever sows sparingly will also reap sparingly, and whoever sows generously will also reap generously" (2 Corinthians 9:6).

Holiness

- "But just as He who called you is holy, so be holy in all you do; for it is written: 'Be holy, because I am holy" (1 Peter 1:15-16).
- "He has saved us and called us to a holy life, not because of anything we have done but because of His own purpose and grace. This grace was given us in Christ Jesus before the beginning of time" (2 Timothy 1:9).
- "Therefore, I urge you, brothers and sisters, in view of God's mercy, to offer your bodies as a living sacrifice, holy and pleasing to God, this is your true and proper worship" (Romans 12:1).
- "Make every effort to live in peace with everyone and to be holy; without holiness no one will see the Lord" (Hebrews 12:14).

Hospitality

- "They must enjoy having guests in their homes and must love all that is good. They must be sensible men, and fair. They must be clean minded and level headed" (Titus 1:8 TLB).
- "Offer hospitality to one another without grumbling" (1 Peter 4:9).
- "Do not forget to show hospitality to strangers, for by so doing some people have shown hospitality to angels without knowing it" (Hebrews 13:2).
- "Share with the Lord's people who are in need. Practise hospitality" (Romans 12:13).

Honouring Others

- "Be devoted to one another in love. Honour one another above yourselves" (Romans 12:10).
- "Honour your father and your mother, as the Lord your God has commanded you, so that you may live long and that it may go well with you in the land the Lord your God is giving you" (Deuteronomy 5:16).
- "Show respect for everyone. Love Christians everywhere. Fear God and honour the government" (1 Peter 2:17 TLB).
- "We are careful to be honourable before the Lord, but we also want everyone else to see that we are honourable" (2 Corinthians 8:21 NLT).

Honesty

- "Honesty guides good people; dishonesty destroys treacherous people" (Proverbs 11:3 NLT).
- "Simply let your 'Yes' be 'Yes' and your 'No' be 'No';

anything beyond this comes from the evil one" (Matthew 5:37 NIV 1984).

- "Righteous lips are the delight of a king, and he loves him who speaks what is right" (Proverbs 16:13 ESV).
- "The Lord detests the use of dishonest scales, but he delights in accurate weights" (Proverbs 11:1 NLT).

Humility

- "Be completely humble and gentle; be patient, bearing with one another in love" (Ephesians 4:2).
- "All of you, clothe yourselves with humility towards one another, because, "God opposes the proud but shows favour to the humble" (1 Peter 5:5b)
- "He guides the humble in what is right and teaches them His way" (Psalms 25:9).
- "For all those who exalt themselves will be humbled, and those who humble themselves will be exalted" (Luke 14:11)

Justice

- "But let justice roll on like a river, righteousness like a never-failing stream!" (Amos 5:24).
- "He has shown you, O mortal, what is good. And what does the Lord require of you? To act justly and to love mercy and to walk humbly with your God" (Micah 6:8).
- "For I, the Lord, love justice; I hate robbery and wrongdoing" (Isaiah 61:8a).
- "Learn to do right; seek justice. Defend the oppressed. Take up the cause of the fatherless;

plead the case of the widow." (Isaiah 1:17)

Kindness

- "Whoever is kind to the poor lends to the Lord, and He will reward them for what they have done" (Proverbs 19:17).
- "Love is patient, love is kind. It does not envy, it does not boast, it is not proud" (1 Corinthians 13:4).
- "Therefore, as God's chosen people, holy and dearly loved, clothe yourselves with compassion, kindness, humility, gentleness and patience" (Colossians 3:12).
- "Be kind and compassionate to one another, forgiving each other, just as in Christ God forgave you" (Ephesians 4:32).

Obedience

- "He replied, "Blessed rather are those who hear the word of God and obey it" (Luke 11:28).
- "And this is love: that we walk in obedience to His commands. As you have heard from the beginning, His command is that you walk in love" (2 John 1:6).
- "And being found in appearance as a man, he humbled himself by becoming obedient to death, even death on a cross!" (Philippians 2:8).
- "Father, if You are willing, take this cup from me; yet not my will, but Yours be done" (Luke 22:42).

Patience

- "A hot-tempered person stirs up conflict, but the one who is patient calms a quarrel" (Proverbs 15:18).
- "The end of a matter is better than its beginning, and patience is better than pride" (Ecclesiastes 7:8).
- "Let us not become weary in doing good, for at the proper time we will reap a harvest if we do not give up" (Galatians 6:9).
- "Be still before the Lord and wait patiently for Him" (Psalm 37:7a)

Peace

- "Do not be anxious about anything, but in every situation, by prayer and petition, with thanksgiving, present your requests to God. And the peace of God, which transcends all understanding, will guard your hearts and your minds in Christ Jesus" (Philippians 4:6-7).
- "Let the peace of Christ rule in your hearts, since as members of one body you were called to peace. And be thankful" (Colossians 3:15).
- "The mind governed by the flesh is death, but the mind governed by the Spirit is life and peace" (Romans 8:6).
- "Blessed are the peacemakers, for they will be called children of God" (Matthew 5:9).

Servanthood

- "For who is greater, the one who is at the table or the one who serves? Is it not the one who is at the table? But I am among you as one who serves" (Luke 22:27).
- "Whoever serves me must follow me; and where I am, my servant also will be. My Father will honour the one who serves me" (John 12:26).
- "Live as free people, but do not use your freedom as a cover-up for evil; live as God's slaves" (1 Peter 2:16).
- "For even the Son of Man came not to be served but to serve, and to give His life as a ransom for many" (Mark 10:45).

Stewardship

- "Each of you should use whatever gift you have received to serve others, as faithful stewards of God's grace in its various forms" (1 Peter 4:10).
- "Whatever you do, work at it with all your heart, as working for the Lord, not for human masters" (Colossians 3:23).
- "If you are faithful in little things, you will be faithful in large ones. But if you are dishonest in little things, you won't be honest with greater responsibilities" (Luke 16:10 NLT).
- "But seek first His kingdom and His righteousness, and all these things will be given to you as well" (Matthew 6:33).

Trustworthiness

- 'The Lord detests lying lips, but He delights in people who are trustworthy" (Proverbs 12:22).
- "Love does not delight in evil but rejoices with the truth" (1 Corinthians 13:6).
- "But blessed is the one who trusts in the Lord, whose confidence is in Him" (Jeremiah 17:7).
- "These are the things you are to do: Speak the truth to each other, and render true and sound judgment in your courts; do not plot evil against each other, and do not love to swear falsely. I hate all this," declares the Lord" (Zechariah 8:16-17).

Unity

- "Again, truly I tell you that if two of you on earth agree about anything they ask for, it will be done for them by my Father in heaven. For where two or three gather in my name, there am I with them" (Matthew 18:19-20).
- "Make every effort to keep the unity of the Spirit through the bond of peace" (Ephesians 4:3).
- "I in them and You in me—so that they may be brought to complete unity. Then the world will know that You sent me and have loved them even as You have loved me" (John 17:23).
- "How good and pleasant it is when God's people live together in unity!" (Psalm 133:1).

Laughter is the closest thing to the grace of God.
Karl Barth

Appendix Four: LIST OF ACTIVITIES

Activity 1: What are Your Natural Gifts?................ 9
Activity 2: Your Personality 19
Activity 3: What Dreams has God Given You? 24
Activity 4: Your Spiritual Gifts 32
Reflection Activity: Your Unique Gifts 33
Activity 5: 40 Days of Prayer for Your Career 51
Activity 6: Your Career Champions.......................... 56
Activity 7: Who is in Your Wider Network? 61
Activity 8: Your Role Models....................................... 68
Reflective Activity: Your Circle of Relationships 70
Activity 9: Your Talent Stories 81
Activity 10: Create Your Skills Bank......................... 91
Activity 11: Complete your Strengths Profile© Online... 102
Reflection Activity: Your Golden Threads............. 105
Activity 12: Your Education Branch 116
Activity 13: Your Knowledge Branch 123
Activity 14: Your Interest Branch 128
Activity 15: Your Compassion Branch 136
Activity 16: What's in Your Inner wisdom?.......... 142
Activity 17: Your Revelations From God................ 149
Reflection Activity: Your Vine Of Curiosity........... 151
Activity 18: Your Career Journey 165
Activity 19: Your STAR Achievements..................... 178
Activity 20: Your CARL Achievements.................... 185
Activity 21: Your Achievements Reviewed........... 186
Activity 22: Identify Your Fruit 192

Activity 23: Your Career Blessings 200
Activity 24: Know Your Values 206
Reflection Activity: Your Career Experience Shield 209
Activity 25: Identifying Your Kingdom Values 223
Activity 26: Your GRACE Displayed 226
Activity 27: Your Career Blueprint 235
Activity 28: Your Career Purpose 239
Reflection Activity: Your Career In God's Hands 241

ACKNOWLEDGEMENTS

I was once asked to choose three words to describe what's important to me. Off the top of my head, I chose **Faith, Family** and **Friends**, without intending any alliteration. These words also provide the framework for my thanks.

Faith, because this is a gift Jesus has given me. Without faith this book wouldn't have been written, not least because Jesus led me every step of the way. Initially it was as if I was literally yoked to Him and His oxen as I tried to furrow my way through the early stages of writing. Then I realised I had become a toddler learning to ride a bike with His steadying hand on the back of the saddle. As I grew in confidence, He stood to the side cheering me on. I will be forever grateful for the idea of this book which He hid in my heart waiting for me to write.

Family, because of the loving framework my family gives me. I am deeply thankful to my husband Mark, who has not only drawn the illustrations for this book, but has painstakingly proof-read it, and cooked and organised for the family whilst I was holed up in my office tapping the keyboard. Heartfelt thanks also to my parents, George and Penelope, who beta-read the book for me, suggested valuable edits and questioned assumptions I'd made. It was with some trepidation that I sent them an early manuscript, but they could not have been more encouraging and supportive.

Finally, thanks to my three children, Oliver, Benjamin and Isabelle who add spice, variety and fun to our family. As they have begun to 'flee the nest' I have had more time to devote to writing this book.

Friends, because without my friends cheering me on this book would not have been written. From the dear Sisters in Christ in my prayer band who knew of my dream many years ago, to friends in my home groups who have prayed through my writing tribulations, and friends I have made recently who have championed me. Many of these people have contributed to this book in the interviews (listed below) and I can count them all as friends. This is especially true of Ladey Adey who has mentored me through the writing process, encouraged me to step out of my comfort zone, dealt with a multitude of final revisions and published the book. Thank you for being a true friend.

I am also indebted to Peter Gray for the fabulous cover picture he designed, and to Gemma Wilks for the lovely brand photos and headshots she took for me.

Peter Gray, www.bigappetiteillustration.com

Gemma Wilks, www.standoutgetnoticed.co.uk

Interviews

My grateful thanks go to the following people who gave up their time to share their career stories and expert advice with me for this book. I loved hearing about their career experiences and am indebted by their openness and support for this book. I hope you have been inspired by their stories and love of Jesus as much as I have been.

Andrea, Client.

Bruce Roberts, Technical Director and Author: *The Godot Orange* www.wordstill.net, facebook.com/timetechteam.

David Davis, Landscape Garden Designer.

Dewi Hughes, Managing Director of Silverlock Tenders www.silverlock.co.uk.

Hanna, Cancer Nurse Specialist.

Jane, an Emotional Health and Wellbeing Consultant for Schools.

Jenny, a recent client.

Ladey Adey, Author: *Successful Business Networking Online*, Speaker, Publisher, for Ladey Adey Publications www.ladeyadey.com.

Lee, a recent client.

Lisa Robertson, Head of Operations, Isaiah 61M www.i61m.org.

Maria, Head of Secondary School and Modern Languages Co-ordinator.

Mark Saxby, Director of Status Social – Social Media with Results www.statussocial.co.uk.

Matt Keown, Painter and Decorator.

Michelle, Actor.

Natasha Chadwick, Consultant and Founder of Impact People and Change, www.impactpeopleandchange.co.uk.

Sue, Doctor.

Sheralyn Pattison, Lawyer and Director of Woofterful® Doggy Daycare and Derby Legal Assistance. Author: *Couch to Kilimanjaro*, https://www.linkedin.com/in/sheralyn-pattison-50947283/.

Grace, like water, flows to the lowest part.
Philip Yancey

REFERENCES AND NOTES

Copyright Page

1. Unless indicated otherwise, Scripture quotations are taken from the ***Holy Bible, New International Version®*** ***Anglicised, NIV®*** Copyright ©1979, 1984, 2011 by Biblica, Inc.® Used by permission. All rights reserved worldwide.

   Scripture quotations marked ***ESV*** are from the ***Holy Bible, English Standard Version. ESV®*** Text Edition: 2016. Copyright ©2001 by Crossway Bibles, a publishing ministry of Good News Publishers. Used by permission. All rights reserved worldwide.

   Scripture quotations marked ***NLT*** are from the ***Holy Bible, New Living Translation***, copyright ©1996, 2004, 2015 by Tyndale House Foundation. Used by permission of Tyndale House Publishers, Inc., Carol Stream, Illinois 60188. All rights reserved.

   Scripture quotations marked ***MSG*** are from ***The Message*** Copyright © 1993, 2002, 2018 by Eugene H. Peterson. Used by permission of NavPress, represented by Tyndale House Publishers. All rights reserved.

   Scripture quotations marked ***NASB*** are from the ***New American Standard Bible®,*** Copyright ©1960, 1971, 1977, 1995, 2020 by The Lockman Foundation. Used by permission. All rights reserved.

   Scripture quotations marked ***TLB*** are from ***The Living Bible*** copyright ©1971 by Tyndale House Foundation. Used by permission of Tyndale House Publishers Inc., Carol Stream, Illinois 60188. All rights reserved.

Introduction

1. Twin Towers - The September 11 attacks, commonly known as 9/11, were a series of four coordinated suicide terrorist attacks carried out in the United States. It included two airplanes flown directly into the World Trade Center North & South Towers (The Twin Towers) causing them to collapse.
2. *The Alpha course* is a course which explains the basics of the Christian faith (https://www.alpha.org).
3. Home Group – a group of 6-12 people who meet in someone's home to study the Bible, consider how it applies to their daily lives and pray together.
4. Julia Yates, *The Career Coaching Handbook* (Routledge; 1st edition, 2013) p.9.
5. Ken Costa, *God at Work: Living Every Day With Purpose* (Alpha International, 2013) p.57.

Chapter One - GIFTS

1. Buzz Lightyear is one of the main characters, alongside Sheriff Woody, in the Toy Story films, produced by Pixar.
2. *NIV Life Application Study Bible* (Hodder & Stoughton: Tyndale House Publishers Inc, revised edition 2011) p.1529.
3. Riding for the Disabled Association (RDA) is a UK based charity providing therapeutic horse riding, equestrian vaulting and carriage driving lessons to people with developmental and physical disabilities as well seeking to improve the lives of those with mental health difficulties.

4. Oxford Learner's Dictionaries (Oxford University Press) www.oxfordlearnersdictionaries.com/definition/english/personality?q=personality accessed 04/11/21.
5. The disciple John wrote *The Gospel of John,* and the letters *1 John* and *2 John*, all found in the New Testament of the Bible.
6. 16personalities.com (NERIS Analytics Limited) www.16personalities.com/free-personality-test accessed 24/11/21.
7. PGCE – A postgraduate certificate in education is an academic qualification which prepares people to become school teachers.
8. ITV – Independent Television - The oldest commercial network in the UK. Today ITV is an integrated producer broadcaster consisting of ITV Studios and Media & Entertainment.
9. Billy Graham's crusades were evangelistic campaigns conducted by Billy Graham across the world between 1947 and 2005.
10. What are Spiritual Gifts? https://www.cru.org/us/en/train-and-grow/spiritual-growth/spiritual-gifts.html accessed 31/05/21.

Chapter Two - RELATIONSHIPS

1. Dave Smith, *God's Plan for Your Wellbeing* (Cwr, 2020) p.123.
2. I used a Stronghold Buster model of prayer for this from *The Freedom In Christ* course. Neil T Anderson and Steve Goss, *Freedom in Christ* (Monarch Books an imprint of Lion Hudson plc, 2009) p 80.
3. Ruth Rice, *Slow Down, Show Up & Pray* (Authentic Media Limited, 2021) p.47.

4. Prayer triplets/fellowship bands https://inspiremovement.org/fellowship-bands accessed 27/09/22.

Chapter Three - ABILITIES

1. Max Lucado, *Cure for the Common Life* (Max Lucado; Reprint edition 2011) p. 7.
2. Nigel Sitwell, edited *The World of Wildlife*, (Hamlyn 1977).
3. Camp America established in 1969 is a cultural exchange programme which gives young people the chance to spend a summer living and working on a summer camp in the USA.
4. John Lees, *How to Get a Job You Love* (UK Higher Education Business Communications 2020) p. 84.
5. Nicky Gumbel, *Bible in One Year* (Alpha International) https://bibleinoneyear.org/en/classic/ accessed 25/02/21.
6. Cappfinity's Strengths Profile® Assessment, www.strengthsprofile.com accessed 16/06/21.

Chapter Four - CURIOSITIES

1. John Lees, *How to Get a Job You Love* (UK Higher Education Business Communications 2020) p. 8.
2. Dyslexia – a learning difficulty which primarily affects the skills involved in accurate and fluent word reading and spelling. www.bdadyslexia.org.uk/dyslexia/about-dyslexia/what-is-dyslexia accessed 29/06/22.
3. Dyscalculia– a specific and persistent difficulty in understanding numbers which can lead to a range of difficulties with mathematics. www.bdadyslexia.org.uk/dyscalculia accessed 29/06/22.

4. Alexander Pope, *Poem*, Literary Devices, (Literary Devices Editors 2013). Metaphor. https://literarydevices.net/a-little-knowledge-is-a-dangerous-thing accessed 23/08/2021.

5. Howard Gardner, *Howard Gardner's Official Authoritative Site of Multiple Intelligences*, (MI Oasis) https://www.multipleintelligencesoasis.org/a-beginners-guide-to-mi accessed 22/06/2021.

6. Howard Gardener, *Existential intelligence*, HowardGardner.com, (©2022 Howard Gardner), www.howardgardner.com/howards-blog/a-resurgence-of-interest-in-existential-intelligence-why-now accessed 21/06/22.

7. *Five Ways to Wellbeing*, (Mind), https://www.mind.org.uk/workplace/mental-health-at-work/taking-care-of-yourself/five-ways-to-wellbeing/ accessed 22/02/2022.

8. *Holland Code*, Wikipedia, (Wikimedia Foundation, Inc) https://en.wikipedia.org/wiki/Holland_Codes accessed 31/05/22.

9. Compassion meaning, Cambridge Dictionary (Cambridge University Press) 2021 https://dictionary.cambridge.org/dictionary/english/compassion accessed 17/11/2021.

10. Etymology of compassion, Wikipedia, (Wikimedia Foundation, Inc https://en.wikipedia.org/wiki/Compassion accessed 17/11/2021.

11. Passion meaning, Cambridge Dictionary, (Cambridge University Press) 2021 https://dictionary.cambridge.org/dictionary/english/passion accessed 17/11/2021.

12. Lectio 365, 24-7 Prayer (24-7 Prayer), 2021 https://www.24-7prayer.com/dailydevotional accessed 12/05/2022.
13. Childline - a counselling service for children and young people up to their 19th birthday in the United Kingdom provided by the NSPCC (National Society for the Prevention of Cruelty to Children).
14. Multiple Sclerosis (MS), a lifelong condition which affects the brain and spinal cord.
15. *Discover Your Life Purpose* ChristianLifeCoaching.co.uk www.christianlifecoaching.co.uk/life-purpose-coaching-program.html accessed 15/06/22.
16. *Discover Your Life Purpose* ChristianLifeCoaching.co.uk Lynne Lee https://www.christianlifecoaching.co.uk/life-purpose-coaching-program.html accessed Oct-2020.
17. International Citizens Service (ICS) is a youth volunteering scheme which brings together young people from the UK and across the world to work together to address poverty and become active global citizens. ICS provides overseas volunteer placements for 18-25 year olds and Team Leader placements for 23-35 year olds.
18. United Christian Broadcasters (UCB) is a Christian media charity which exists to offer every person, in every place, every moment of the day, the opportunity to hear, watch or read the Word of God in a relevant and engaging way. It operates radio and television stations and publishes and broadcasts Bob Gass's free daily devotionals The Word for You Today and Word For You. https://www.ucb.co.uk/
19. Pete Greig, *How to Hear God - A Simple Guide for Normal People* (Hodder & Stoughton 2022) p.194.

Chapter Five – EXPERIENCES

1. Søren Kierkegaard *Life can only be lived backwards* Everyday-inspirationalquotes.com https://www.everyday-inspirational-quotes.com/life-can-only-be-understood-backwards-but-it-must-be-lived-forwards/ accessed 11/09/2022
2. Lehman Brothers went bankrupt on 15th September 2008 leading to the collapse of the financial and investment banking system and subsequent recession.
3. Lexico.com (Oxford University Press) https://www.lexico.com/definition/achievement accessed 29/06/2021.
4. PGCE – A postgraduate certificate in education is an academic qualification which prepares people to become school teachers.
5. TEFL – the acronym for teaching English as a foreign language or English language instruction for non-native speakers.
6. Confucius Institute - public educational and cultural promotion programmes funded and arranged by the Chinese International Education Foundation.
7. Sister Programme - In November 2017, Maria with a delegation from Nottingham University together with the Confucius Institute signed a sister school agreement with a school in Ningbo to commit to organise an exchange between the two schools which took place April 2019.
8. The International School Award rewards schools that have shown a commitment to embedding international awareness and understanding within their class or school. https://www.britishcouncil.org/school-resources/accreditation/international-school-award/about accessed 16/08/22.

9. Hanna is originally from Finland. "Finnish guts" is her terminology for persisting, rather than a generalisation about all people from Finland.
10. The University of Edinburgh (The University of Edinburgh, 2018) https://www.ed.ac.uk/reflection/reflectors-toolkit/reflecting-on-experience/carl accessed 29/06/2021.
11. Susan J Nelson, *Woman of Noble Character*, https://www.womanofnoblecharacter.com/fruits-in-the-bible/ accessed 01/06/22.
12. In the English Fairy Story, *Jack and the Beanstalk,* Jack plants some magic beans which grow into a huge beanstalk overnight.
13. Roy Godwin, *The Way of Blessing* (David C Cook 2016) p.160-161.
14. Parochial Church Council – the governing body of a parish church, made up of members of the clergy and congregation to oversee the church's charitable works, finances and governance.

Chapter Six – GOD'S GRACE FOR YOU

1. Neil T Anderson and Steve Goss, *Freedom in Christ* (Monarch Books an imprint of Lion Hudson plc, 2009) p. 72.
2. Nicky Gumbel, *Bible in One Year, -Day 314* (Alpha International) https://bibleinoneyear.org/en/classic accessed 23 Nov 2021.
3. Paul Bulkeley, *The BizMin Course* (Bizmin, 2020) p. 97.

Appendix One.

1. Your SHAPE for God's Service, Amiel Mary E.Osmaston (Arthur Rank Centre)

https://arthurrankcentre.org.uk/resources/your-shape-for-gods-service/your-shape-for-gods-service-full-course-2013-version/ accessed 31/05/2021 3rd Edition.

2. Erik Rees, S.H.A.P.E: Finding and Fulfilling Your Unique Purpose in Life (Zondervan) 2006.

ABOUT THE AUTHOR

Katie Conley

Engaging, dedicated, insightful - this is how Katie's clients describe her and the career coaching she offers. Katie is a licensed Career Coach, accredited Strengths Profile© practitioner, a registered professional with the Career Development Institute and an associate member of the Chartered Institute of Personnel and Development.

Throughout her varied career the times she's enjoyed the most are when she has been talking with people about what they do and why! Katie has managed graduate recruitment programmes, delivered career development workshops, created personal development plans, provided career coaching and delivered lots of skills development training. She's been a sales assistant, waitress, training officer, head of department, non-exec director and director of her own learning and development consulting business, all of which has brought her into contact with a wide range of people. She has always been keen to learn about the choices people make for their working lives and help them make changes, learn new things, or take on new challenges.

She set up *Conley Career Coaching* to specifically continue her passion for helping people progress in their careers, whether this is helping them make choices for their next career move or helping someone back into work following a career break, discussing career options, putting together a job search strategy, advising on CVs or doing some interview practice.

Katie has been a Christian for over 20 years. She has a certificate in Christian Discipleship and oversees home groups for her church, as well as running two of them. She has led several Alpha courses (for those exploring the Christian faith) and is also on the prayer ministry team. Katie is very comfortable discussing career choices from a Christian viewpoint and loves to see how our faith interacts with our career choices and what God has planned for us.

She would love to hear your experiences too!

Contact Katie directly via these links:

www.conleycareercoaching.com/

linkedin.com/in/katieconley-careercoach/

facebook.com/conleycareercoaching

twitter.com/ConleyCareers

www.instagram.com/katieconleycareercoach/

Career Coaching Options

Career Clarity

Be clear about your career direction.

- The path to career clarity is different for everyone and tailored to your specific needs. This series of 1-to-1 personalised coaching always involves a voyage of self-discovery to help you unpack your career toolkit so you can be clear about what you've got followed by visioning your future career, assessing your resources and making a career plan.

Clients gain increased confidence in their future career options.

Career Change

Don't leave your career change to chance!

- If you're serious about making a career change and determined to invest the time and effort required, then over a few months you will undertake a thorough and detailed exploration of what you want and discover how to take steps to achieve your vision for your future career.

Clients will be equipped with practical ideas and know the steps to take to realise their career dreams.

Job Search

Gain confidence in your job search.

- Not everyone enjoys job searching, and many people don't know where to start. Designed around you, job search coaching includes support and advice on the job search process including job search strategy, creating an up-to-date relevant CV/LinkedIn profile, networking, the application process and preparing for interviews.

Clients will be able to search for a new job with confidence and courage.

Christian Career Coaching

Explore career options from a faith perspective.

- Explore and discuss your career choices and challenges from a Christian perspective with space to pray and discern God's purpose and plans for your career. Many Christians find it really helpful to be able to discuss their career from a Christian perspective without feeling they have to censor their words or thoughts.

Contact Katie for a free 1-1 consultation to see how she can help you.

I am not what I ought to be.
I am not what I want to be.
I am not what I hope to be.
But still, I am not what I used to be.
And by the grace of God, I am what I am.

John Newton

INDEX

Symbols

16personalities.com 283

A

Aaron 90
Adam and Eve 194, 195
Adams, Thomas viii
Adey, Ladey vi, xxi, 58, 59, 61, 278, 279
Adoption 134
Alpha Course xviii, 282
Amazon's Alexa 117
Anderson, Neil T 283, 288
Andrea, Teacher 21, 278
Apostle John 12, 283
Apostle Paul 42, 57, 64, 65, 113, 188, 244
Apostle Peter 11, 113, 219
Apple's Siri 117
Ark of the Covenant 83, 86
Armed Forces 217

B

Barnabas 64, 65
Barth, Karl 274
Bateman, Trudy iii
Bert - Driving Instructor 76
Bezalel 84, 89, 90
Briggs, Katherine 13
Bulkeley, Paul 288
Buzz Lightyear 282

C

Cambridge Dictionary 129
Camp America 284
Career Clarity 293
Career Development Institute 291
CARL Model 184
Central Television 171
Chadwick, Natasha xxi, 139, 141, 279
Childline 132, 133, 147, 286
Christian Career Coaching 294
Confucius Institute 287
Costa, Ken xxi, 282
Covid-19 Pandemic 58, 148

D

Davis, David xx, xxi, 7, 65, 115, 121, 122, 133, 146, 190, 278
Deborah 41

E

Eareckson Tada, Joni 242
English Fairy Story 288

F

Facebook 61, 62, 68
Finney, Charles 262
Finn, Frances iv

G

Garden of Gethsemane 53
Gardner, Howard 118, 121, 122, 285
Gideon 26
Godwin, Roy 194, 288
Goliath 86
Goss, Steve 218, 283, 288
Graham, Billy 23, 283
Gray, Peter vi, 278, 279
Greig, Pete 146, 286
Gumbel, Nicky 90, 219, 284, 288

H

Haman 99
Hanna - Nurse xxi, 179, 180, 181, 183, 279, 288
Holland Code 285
Holland, John L 125
Hughes, Dewi xxi, 160, 161, 162, 205, 206, 278

I

Independent Television 283
Instagram 61, 62, 68
International Citizens Service (ICS) 140, 286
International School Award 287

J

Jacob 195
Jane xxi
Jane - Consultant for Schools 131, 133, 147, 148, 279
Jenny - Client 89, 96, 279
Joanna 53
Job Search Coaching 294
John the Baptist 94
Jonah 41, 42
Joseph 157, 160, 165, 187, 195
Jung, Carl 13

K

Keown, Matt xxi, 80, 163, 197, 279
Kierkegaard, Søren 155, 287
King Artaxerxes 168, 170
King David xx, 5, 6, 7, 85
King Saul 5, 85, 86
King Solomon 110

L

Lazarus 53
Lectio 365 132, 286
Lee - Client 101, 279
Lee, Lynne 138, 286
Lees, John 83, 109, 284
Lego® 225
Lehman Brothers 164, 287
Lewis, C S 219
Licensed Career Coach 291
LinkedIn 61, 62, 68
Lockdown 2020 27
Lucado, Max 78, 284

M

Magdalene, Mary 53
Mair, Marjory iv
Maria - Secondary School Teacher xxi, 8, 173, 177, 198, 200, 279, 287
Martha 53
Mary 53
Mental health 134
Michelle - Actor xxi, 22, 49, 50, 279
Moses 48, 90
Multiple Sclerosis 132, 133, 148, 286
Myers Briggs Type Indicator 13, 17
Myers, Isabel 13

N

Nathan (Prophet) 98
Nathan, Rob ii
Natural History Museum 78
Nehemiah 168, 169, 170
Nelson, Susan J 288
New Economics Foundation 124
Newton, John xi, 296
Noah 48

O

Oholiab 84
Osmaston, Amiel Mary E 248, 288
Othniel 26

P

Palmer, Stuart iii
Parfitt, Matt iii
Parochial Church Council 288
Pattison, Sheralyn xxi, 28, 29, 30, 133, 280
PGCE 21, 283, 287
Pope, Alexander 117, 285
Potiphar 158, 187, 195
Premier Christian Radio 45
Prodigal Son xiv, xv, 39, 43, 243
Proudlove, Lee Revd 248

Q

Queen Elizabeth II 214
Queen Esther 98

R

Rees, Erik 248, 289
RIASEC 125, 127
Rice, Ruth ii, 41, 283
Riding for the Disabled Association 6, 282
Roberts, Bruce xxi, 13, 14, 15, 16, 17, 278
Robertson, Lisa 48, 50, 279
Royal Air Force 59
Ruth 94

S

Samson 26, 94
Samuel 94
Saxby, Mark vi, xxi, 43, 44, 45, 46, 48, 277, 279
Seekers 134
Sister Programme 287
Sitwell, Nigel 284
Smith, Dave 283
Spidergram 61, 62, 63, 70
STAR Framework 169, 177, 184
Strengths Profile Assessment 284
Sue - Doctor xxi, 23, 24, 54, 65, 66, 99, 100, 114, 279
Suzanna 53

T

TEFL 287
Time Magazine xv
Tozer, A W 300
Twin Towers xv, 282
Twitter 61, 62, 68

U

United Christian Broadcasters 145, 286
University of Edinburgh 288

W

Whyte, Alexander xii
Wilks, Gemma vi, 278, 279
World Wildlife Fund 79

Y

Yancey, Philip
Yates, Julia xxi, 282
Yearsley, Tim ii
Yorkie® Bar 76
Yorkshire Post 45
Youth Mental Health First Aid 132
Youth Training Scheme (YTS) 115
YouTube 125

Z

Zoom® 58, 60

The grace of God is infinite
and beyond our ability to measure.
His grace has no beginning
and therefore no end.

A W Tozer

YOUR NOTES

A few pages for you to make your own notes.

Your Notes

Your Notes

A PRAYER FOR YOUR CAREER

Heavenly Father

Thank You for Your **GRACE** for my career, for the clues You have hidden for me, the insight You have equipped me with and Your continual guidance.

Thank You for my gifts, both natural and spiritual, for my personality and my career dreams. Help me to identify the gifts You want me to use in my career.

Thank You for my relationships, especially with You - so deep and personal. Help me to trust You day by day for my career choices. Thank You for my trusted friends, my wider network and the role models who go before me.

Thank You for the many abilities You have given me, for my talents, skills, and strengths. Help me to clarify the ones that are relevant for me now.

Thank You for my curiosities. Help me to take a deep dive into my education, knowledge, and interests, to recognise my compassions and inner wisdom, and reveal to me promises for my career.

Thank You for my career experiences. Help me to recognise my achievements, the fruit You are growing in me, the ways You bless me and illuminate my values.

As I unwrap all the **GRACE** You have given me, help me to recognise my career blueprint, pin-point my career purpose and see Your loving grace at work in my career.

In Jesus name, Amen

Ingram Content Group UK Ltd.
Milton Keynes UK
UKHW020812020523
420994UK00008B/84